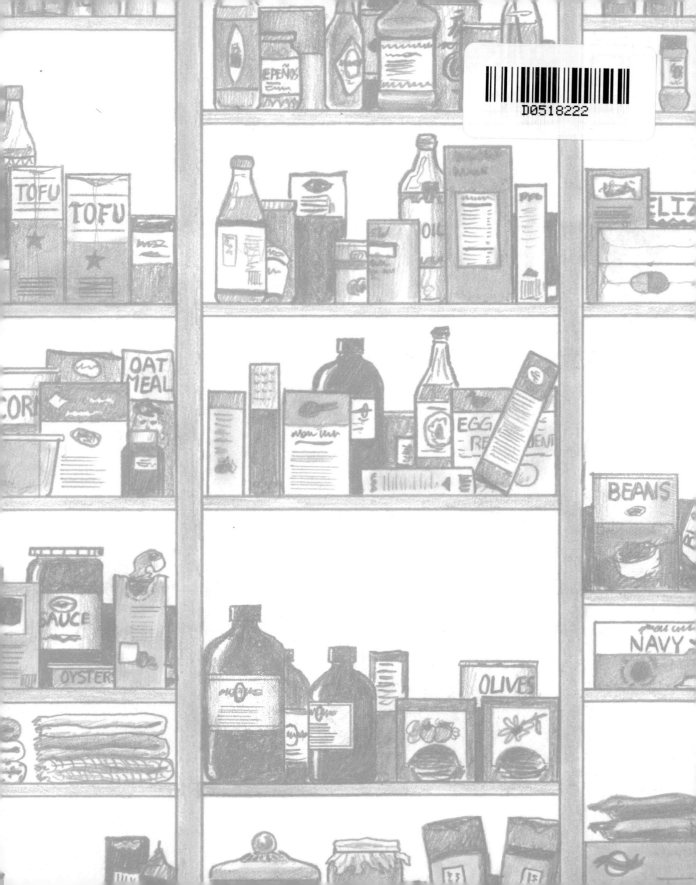

GRAHAM KERR'S

Swiftly Seasoned

Other Books by Graham Kerr

Graham Kerr's Smart Cooking

Graham Kerr's Minimax™ Cookbook

Graham Kerr's Creative Choices Cookbook

Graham Kerr's Kitchen

Graham Kerr's Best

GRAHAM KERR'S

Swiftly Seasoned

Graham Kerr

G. P. PUTNAM'S SONS
NEW YORK

G. P. Putnam's Sons
Publishers Since 1838
200 Madison Avenue
New York, NY 10016

Copyright ©1996 by Kerr Corporation

Library of Congress Cataloging-in-Publication Data

Kerr, Graham.
  [Swiftly seasoned]
  Graham Kerr's swiftly seasoned.
    p. cm.
  ISBN 0-399-14243-6
    1. Cookery.   2. Low-fat diet—Recipes.   3. Quick and easy cookery.
  I. Title.
  TX714.K486 1997   96-288777 CIP
  641.5'638—dc20

Printed in the United States of America
        1 2 3 4 5 6 7 8 9 10

This book is printed on acid-free paper. ∞

Book design by H. Roberts Design

Acknowledgments:
The finest seasonings a cook can have

Contents

Preface

Twenty-two is important to me. I was born on January 22, Treena and I married on September 22, and our first daughter, Tessa, was born on September 22 (one year later)! I could easily add a myriad of other important events, including this book; it's my twenty-second! I believe that it represents a major milestone because it aims at combining three vital present-day needs: great taste, good health, and swift preparation.

I have used five major elements in this all-new collection of recipes. They guide everything I've sought to achieve for you, your family, and your friends.

1. <u>**SEASONING:**</u> It has been said that success in the retail business is "location, location, location." In my mind, success in the kitchen is "seasoning, seasoning, seasoning." I've set out to provide *swift* ways to get superb layered flavors in every single recipe. This aromatic benefit is especially vital when creating recipes that use less fat, salt, and sugar as well as smaller portions of meat.
2. <u>**MEATLESS MEALS:**</u> There is an enormous interest in occasional vegetable-only meals. Yet when the meat is missing, the plate often loses its familiar focus. I have used simple ethnic food combinations, well seasoned, to create a new focus and much greater enjoyment. I've called these MEVs (for Molded Ethnic Vegetables). You'll find sixteen variations on what I hope will be a popular new theme.
3. <u>**FUTURE FOODS—TODAY?:**</u> "New" is a much-abused word. However, some foods are emerging in "new" forms that are healthful and full of flavor, and can be swiftly cooked. Whilst some foods are still expensive, there is reason to believe that when they become more popular, the price will fall rapidly (remember the VCR?). I'll tell you about ostrich, bison (buffalo), venison—all low-fat red meats—and low-sodium, organic, cooked beans as well as a truly low-fat firm tofu.
4. <u>**FRUIT ON FRUIT FOR DESSERT:**</u> I've assembled fresh fruit in flavor partnerships and suggested great seasonings and simple cooking or presentation techniques as well as each fruit's prime season and best variety. These ideas are *swift*, elegant, wonderfully varied, and abound in good taste and good health.
5. <u>**BY EVERY MODERN MEANS:**</u> More than 40 percent of all North American households now have personal computers. We live in the midst of a domestic technological age. We are used to pushing buttons to get things done. Not all machines really help; some speed the process but spoil the end product. Throughout the text of this book I've included, where appropriate, expanded comments and illustrations that will help you decide if low-tech and high-tech appliances will help you be more successful in the kitchen in less time.

GRAHAM KERR'S

Swiftly Seasoned

Introduction

What Is Swift?

*S*wift isn't merely fast. A jet is fast; a bird is swift. The apparent ease with which a swallow turns reveals the mechanical stress of its fast, flashy fellow flier. In this book I shall try to present what I have come to see as the apparent ease that I call *swift*.

Speed and swiftness are not the same thing at all. Speed assumes that the priority is convenience—a feature readily available in every food store with mass-production frozen dinners, deli dishes, and packaged entrees. Swiftness calls for simple ways to provide a meal that meets our individual needs.

In an almost lemminglike manner, many modern consumers have rushed forward to embrace the minute-by-minute savings proposed by advertisements, often to find that they've saved time at the expense of taste and cost.

Is time really that important? Could

swift *ease of preparation* meet our pressured need and still allow for good taste, aroma, color, texture, nutrition, and *not* bash the budget?

Food preparation becomes *fast* when almost everything is cooked for you in bulk and then preserved so that all you need to do is reheat and eat. Cooking becomes *swift* when some of your effort is facilitated *by every modern means*, by equipment that replaces some of the repetitive time-consuming labor with smart machines like those that mix and bake your chosen bread recipe when *you* want it. Wrapped sliced bread is faster but it can't compete with the aroma, the taste, and the pure nutritional content which are possible from your very own selected bread recipe.

"Aha!" I hear you say. "But what of the *cost* of these smart machines that make the difference?" It's true that there are capital expenditures to equip the *swift* kitchen, and taken all at once they could appear formidable. But please remember that many of the well-made modern appliances can last a lifetime and provide good health *and* pleasure for your family and friends for years. A well-designed, modern kitchen helps to keep the idea of creative cooking alive in a time when life itself appears dominated by convenience in its need for speed.

You don't need everything at once

Let me explain how it can work: You get home tired, even exhausted, and the family wants to eat. First, slip some sweet potatoes into the microwave oven on high. You pass a variety of washed root vegetables through the food processor. Add a touch of oil to a second-generation stainless steel pressure cooker. Then stir the vegetables to release flavor oils. Add canned (or frozen) stock and swift seasoning, rice, lentils—all can be your choices.

Now pressure-cook for about six minutes whilst you heat the plates and rinse out the food processor. "Time's up!" Release the pressure from the cooker. Pour out your own creative minestrone into deep bowls and dust with a little Parmesan cheese. Cut some crusty bread. "Beep!" The potatoes are ready. . . . let's eat!

200 typical housewives

That process took twenty minutes. The food you used was fresh. It was your choice of favorite ingredients, not based on a food manufacturer's survey of two hundred typical housewives. You know you are not "typical"—nobody is! We are all individuals. I don't see myself as a statistic. I'm a person with preferences who just took ten minutes more to *cook* rather than *reheat*. It was easier because the same soup and potatoes would take nearly an hour without the modern means.

I refuse to be a statistic

That's the basic difference! When I have the equipment and my preferred swift seasoning, I'm investing an extra ten minutes to replace canned soup. But without the modern means that ease the task, I face the possibility of spending thirty to forty minutes to do it. That fact could possibly motivate me to choose to reheat someone else's preseasoned, precooked food or to buy a pizza on the way home.

investing 10 minutes to replace canned soup

Day after day of this sort of "speed cooking" seems to reinforce the idea that to cook is boring and unrewarding (when the truth is that you are missing the personal, individual little seasoning touches that make *your* food *yours*, and make cooking a genuine act of creative kindness to those you love). Please don't trade the apparent ease of *swift* for the flashy, mechanical stress of *fast!*

Now, is the investment worth it? Only you can answer the question.

cooking is boring

To help you make an informed decision, I have discussed important features about the equipment throughout this book that can be used to some advantage for both time and quality.

Swift-er Seasoning

During a recent world tour, I interviewed chefs and collected recipes for an upcoming Public Television series. Over a period of four months, I visited master herb and spice merchants in Singapore, Bombay, Mombasa, Aqaba, Jerusalem, and, of all places, Sydney, Australia.

Fresh and Best in season

Everywhere I went there was a strong resurgence of what I call FABIS, an acronym for *Fresh And Best In Season*, in which climate, culture, and classic seasonings combine to create a unique regional flavor.

There is a renewed interest in micronationalism, which is a passion for one's home and a yearning for

I call it Northern Fried Chicken

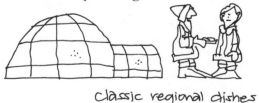

classic regional dishes

others to notice the regional differences that are worthy of attention. Food is simply one facet of this expression, which, like music, is available throughout a community and shapes its culture.

North Americans have emerging regional seasonings related to climate and history. The pungent Creole and Cajun cuisines are good examples, but elsewhere we remain more influenced by our own melting-pot backgrounds than climate and we are regionally diffused. As the micronational renewal heats up, we North Americans increasingly want to identify with our ancestors. As a result, we are about to see a flood of interest in *authentically seasoned* international dishes which can meet our North American criteria for ease of preparation and good health. This means that ethnic spice and herb combinations will play a huge role in the development of our own regional food styles.

I call herb and spice combinations Ethmix™ for *ethnic mixtures*. The home cook can, of course, measure and combine the readily available individual herbs and spices in accord with the guidance of a reputable author, but there are three small stumbling blocks to this method.

The first is that many of our home-stored herbs and spices are older (weaker) than we'd like to admit. Just one out-of-date seasoning can spoil the entire mix. Second comes the appearance of dried herbs: thyme, rosemary, and basil, for example, can wind up looking as though you've used tea leaves unless they are bound up in muslin or in a steel mesh ball. Finally, there is the specific weight difference between herbs and spices that can result in "shake down," with greater spice intensity at the bottom of the jar. Because of all three reasons, freshly powdered well-blended combinations prefer to be used within a year of their making.

Alas, we North Americans are now so inundated with messages telling us we are out of time that we hasten to uncover every wasted second in the kitchen. Confronted with a new recipe, the pressured cook tends to pale when the ingredient list exceeds eight or more items in total. Therefore, a list of multiple herbs and spices is likely to bring about instant rejection of a dish when in fact, it's the layers of balanced flavors that really help to creatively replace unhealthy amounts of fat, salt, and refined carbohydrates.

What a pity! However, this is where the carefully balanced ethmixes work so well, because regardless of the number of ingredients contained, each special collection now equals just *one recipe item*.

My Peripatetic Swiftly Seasoned Pantry

Understand me, my pantry does not "walk about," which is the literal meaning of *peripatetic*. It is I who walk about, endlessly seeking out ways to season my food so that I can get continued variety without the fat, salt, and refined carbohydrates that we've been so accustomed to using.

Years ago, I went through an anti-clutter phase in which everything had its

graham's peripatetic pantry

frozen food manufacturer it was discovered that the great majority of home cooks wait until the last moment before deciding what to eat for their evening meal. It seems to me that an on-display pantry would prompt adventurous souls to add a dash of ethnic spice to their frozen chicken entree and, as a result, regain a whisper of their creative feelings from when they had the time (or inclination?) to cook from scratch.

Armed with such a pantry you will be certain that your seasonings will be swifter, more assured of success, and ultimately a great joy for your household and for your friends.

Whole Foods for the Future

Every cookbook author hopes that his or her book will be around for years to come, and occasionally I feel that some of my past ideas have been ahead of their time. In a small subsection of this book, I've introduced you to just six "future" foods. Each is on the market, some are still quite expensive, but all six have their own potential to become popular because they meet our goals for both healthful and swift cooking.

Three of the future foods are red meats—venison, bison (also called buffalo), and ostrich. All three are really low in fat yet all have excellent appeal to the red meat eater in color, texture, tenderness, and taste.

The other introductions are an eclectic assortment. Farmed catfish provide a healthy alternative to fish being caught in areas of agricultural runoff and industri-

put-away place. I declared with some passion that I would prefer to work inside a blown eggshell. Recently I've taken to putting my pantry on display. I don't mean to flaunt the contents of my pantry like a kitchen version of leather-bound sets of encyclopedias or the Great Classics that are never read, but rather as a spontaneous selection facilitator. It has become a kind of artist's palette in bottles, jars, and packages from which I can gain inspiration just by letting my eyes rove peripatetically from label to label. (On the front and back endpapers of this book artist Mark Zelmer's representation of the idea of a *seasoning wall* shows you what I mean.)

My newly exposed pantry with all of its swift seasonings does have the appearance of clutter, but somehow it fits with our love of good food and the international nature of what we do. It also lends greatly to the comfort factor.

In a recent survey made by a giant

al wastes. Beans in several varieties are now being grown organically and canned with much less sodium content. This is very good news for the swift pantry (see page 46) because of the many other health and flavor benefits that are derived from beans' fiber content. Finally tofu, often underappreciated, has become conveniently available in aseptic pouches that need no refrigeration until opened—once again a great opportunity for the pantry. Better yet, the tofu comes in degrees of firmness and in reduced fat levels.

I don't believe for a moment that this will be the end of what will happen in the future. My only hope is that we will keep on preferring to use *real* foods from the purest sources possible. I'm old-fashioned enough to believe that *fake* will never truly compete with *fresh*.

Meatless Meals

Whilst on the word *fresh*, a brief word about the mainstream movement to increase the number of meatless menus we include in our everyday cooking. I specifically use the term *meatless* rather than *vegetarian* because my purpose here is to focus upon reducing the negative effects of saturated animal fats rather than advocating the adoption of some level of vegetarian lifestyle.

I'm convinced that very few people count fat grams every day. What often happens is that we monitor ourselves for a short time until we get a general feel for the amount of fat we can tolerate. Then perhaps we eat something a little

high on the hog, like a wedge of fresh Brie, some crusty French bread and good butter with a chilled juicy ripe pear. We will then compensate the next day by reducing animal fats. We may even make the entire day meatless.

This method works, to some degree, but it's likely to get out of hand if we use these animal fat–free days as a kind of movable Lent, designed to soak up deliberate excesses. I suggest that it is wiser to plan, for instance, that alternate days be meatless and let the naturally low fat and high fiber add fresh benefit and variety.

Throughout this book, I've tried hard to replace the meat, poultry, and fish focus by building a new point of interest: the molded ethnic vegetable (MEV). The MEV is characterized by layers of complementary vegetables and starches, appropriately spiced and molded—a technique reminiscent of shaped gelatin salads or desserts—that provides a visual as well as physical focus to any plate. I have devoted a large section of this book and my companion "Swiftly Seasoned" television program to this whole idea. See pages 117–125.

Fruit on Fruit

On a visit to the fruit wonderland of New Zealand in 1987, I visited an orchard in the Bay of Plenty in the North Island. As we sampled several excellent varieties of tree-ripened fruit, I literally fell into an extraordinary taste sensation.

The watery crisp/sweet *nashi* (also called a Japanese or Asian pear) are nearly round, pale yellow, apple-sized, and often found in the market individually wrapped in a latticed foam net. Immediately after tasting a slice of the nashi, I ate a wedge of fresh-picked nectarine still warm

Graham discovers fruit on fruit

from the sun. The combination was almost electric. I repeated it with a slice of each together. Later, I made a swift blender purée of the nectarine and laid a freshly cut crisp nashi on this tart-sweet golden bed. It was delicious, and with that simple act I had discovered the creative joy of *fruit on fruit* for the easiest and most attractive of desserts. Beginning on page 182 I've given you my experience of which blends are best along with some tricks and tips for preparation and serving.

It really is great fun, truly creative, and *so easy*. Don't let my list hold you back from your own unique combinations. I'd love to hear if you've struck flavor "gold." My address, as always, is in the back of the book.

Fresh-Food Fun Factory

Let's face it—not everyone is going to cook from scratch every day. So what is the fallback position, and are you happy with your present solution?

Here's a typical scenario: You've had a long, hard day. You *want* comfort, you *need*

comfort, and it's entirely reasonable that you will try very hard to get it. The commercial food industry knows this about you—and millions like you—so they are ready and waiting. You could swing by the pizza palace, the burger joint, the Chinese takeout, or your neighborhood coffee shop.

Or, you might pick up dinner from the frozen food section of your supermarket: entrees or whole meals—including vegetable and dessert—cunningly packaged in segmented trays ready to pop into the oven or microwave.

Everyone is ready to send you home with dinner!

You're home, you light a fire (or flip a switch), turn on the telly, sink down into your favorite chair, and dig in. You're drowsy but entertained; the heat and the food spell *comfort*.

If one of these has been your solution to feeding yourself or your family at the end of the day, then I'm guessing that it's not a standard operating procedure; otherwise, *you wouldn't be reading this book.*

If you're one of many who has managed to avoid outside influence and has extra meals prepared in advance, frozen, and ready for action, I want to encourage you in this endeavor. I have written about this idea in one of my previous books, *Graham Kerr's Kitchen*, but now I'd like to take this notion one step further and propose that you turn your kitchen into a *Fresh-Food Fun Factory* once a week for two to four hours.

This will be more fun if you can persuade the family (or friends) to join you in the process. It will certainly take some organization to give everyone a specific task, a place, and the equipment with which to work. But given those things plus the right size deep freeze and a commitment once a week for two to four hours, it will mean that you've always got freshly made, familiar, freshly frozen food, for frequent facilitated fat-free (and here I ran out of words beginning with f!) evening meals on those days when you're so tired that you just want to "flop out"!

As a guide to setting up the factory, may I repeat my advice concerning the use of the deep freeze for *frozen* flat foods filed for future use! (I didn't run out, after all.)

• Pack it flat. I use heavy-duty reclosable bags. (I use Ziploc bags because they are strong and easy to seal.) Use a size that meets your needs, exhaust the air, seal, and then freeze flat.

• Cool the food quickly before you freeze it. Don't let the food items lie

around before freezing. They will continue to cook, perhaps ruin a perfectly crisp texture. Put the ingredients in your reclosable bag, seal it, and then cool it in very cold water or over ice cubes before freezing.

• Note the date. Cooked food deteriorates faster than uncooked food, losing its color, flavor, and texture. So please date each bag with a description and use it within six months.

• Frozen menu: Keep an extra bag on which you just write down the names of what you are freezing. Keep the erasable pen in the bag with spare bags of various sizes. It will be your reminder of what you have and when you need to use it.

• Some food doesn't freeze well. The higher the fat content, the shorter its storage potential. Raw tomatoes don't freeze well at all and salad vegetables, especially greens, get mushy, while milk and yogurt sauces will curdle.

• Don't overdo the quantity. Your freezer can accept no more than 2 pounds (900 gm) of food per cubic foot of its capacity. Thus, a 3-cubic-foot deep freeze can efficiently hold no more than 6 pounds (2.7 kg) of food at any one time.

• Defrost carefully. Frozen foods spoil faster than freshly cooked and cooled. Don't ever let food sit at room temperature for over three hours to thaw.

• Thaw overnight in the refrigerator. To be safe, I allow my bags to gradually thaw in the refrigerator (think ahead!) or I microwave them for 6 to 8 minutes for each 1 pound (450 gm) of food at the 30 power setting (the usual power used for the defrost cycle).

Try for a perfect marriage! Remember that your fun food will gradually lose its flavor over a limited six-month freezing period. Therefore, when you use it, marry it to fresh fruit, vegetables, pasta, and whole grains, seasoned with the very best condiments that will enhance aroma, color, and texture.

Soups
and
Salads

Swift Soups

I am absolutely convinced that soup and bread can become at least a once-a-week special in the modern home and be greatly appreciated by everyone. If you combine the pressure cooker (or a perfectly acceptable, but slower, regular saucepan) and a bread machine (or make friends with a great local baker who does real bread), you can get genuinely swift soups and a home filled with aromas! This beats takeout or "nuked" frozen entrees any day.

Freshness and individual creativity can be let loose in this incredible opportunity for both variety and seasonings. Here are a couple of ideas for swift soups and a plea that you turn to page 171 and have a look at my crusty bread.

Oh, by the way, it's great fun to have a Soup 'n Bread party. All you do is ask your best pals to bring a quarter pound of vegetables or grain or pasta per head (their heads, not yours)! When your guests arrive, they cut the vegetables and you add them according to cooking times, holding back the pastas and leafy vegetables until the end. Let each person bring home-baked bread in a large Ziploc bag, so that what isn't eaten can go back home again. You, as the host, prepare a truly excellent poultry- or vegetable-based broth—enough for 10 fluid ounces per guest (this allows for some evaporation during cooking).

I like to set out an herb-seasoned yogurt cheese, some interesting cheeses that include lower-fat varieties, or some of my special bean dips. Good local wine or beers—in my case Ariél de-alcoholized wines and Kaliber or Coors de-alcoholized beers—go very well with the breads, cheeses, and sumptuous soup to which everyone has made a contribution.

Tomato Vegetable Soup with Sweet Potato

Serves 4

4 small sweet potatoes
1 teaspoon light olive oil with a dash of toasted sesame oil
1 onion, cut in quarters and sliced
2 cloves garlic, peeled, bashed, and chopped
3 tablespoons plus 3 cups no-salt-added tomato juice
1 (15½-ounce or 432 gm) can low-sodium red kidney beans
1 cup frozen corn
1/4 teaspoon salt
1½ teaspoons Bali Spice Mix (page 218)
12 leaves fresh cilantro, chopped

Garnish
4 tablespoons yogurt cheese (page 210)
4 tablespoons chopped cilantro leaves

Microwave the sweet potatoes until soft, 10 minutes or more on high.

Preheat a large saucepan with the oil and add the onions and garlic and cook for 1 minute. Pull the onions and garlic to one side and add 3 tablespoons of tomato juice, one at a time, to the other side of the pan, reducing each to a dark paste before adding the next. Stir into the onions and garlic, add the remaining tomato juice, kidney beans, corn, and the salt and cook over low heat for 5 minutes. Add seasoning mix. Slice the sweet potatoes crosswise into 3/4-inch (2-cm) rounds, then cut with a round scalloped cookie cutter and drop into the soup. Add the cilantro.

To serve: Ladle into a bowl, top with a dollop of yogurt cheese, and garnish with the chopped cilantro. Serve with Whole Wheat Quinoa Bread (page 173).

Time Estimate: Preparation, 15 minutes; cooking, 20 minutes

Nutritional Profile per Serving: Calories—371; % calories from fat—8%; fat (gm)—3 or 5% daily value; saturated fat (gm)—0; sodium (mg)—248; cholesterol (mg)—0; carbohydrates (gm)—74; dietary fiber (gm)—12; protein (gm)—16. Analysis includes suggested side dishes.

North African Pea Soup with a Couscous MEV

This recipe introduces the MEV, an acronym for Molded Ethnic Vegetables, which I've fully explained beginning on page 117.

Serves 4

Soup
1¼ cups dried yellow split peas
5 cups low-sodium vegetable stock (page 210)
1 teaspoon harissa (page 219), divided
1 clove garlic, peeled, bashed, and chopped
2 medium turnips, peeled and diced
16 tiny onions, peeled
6 mustard green, turnip green, or kale leaves,
    rolled and cut in thin strips
1 sprig (4-inch or 10-cm) fresh rosemary

MEV
1⅓ cups couscous
1/8 teaspoon salt
2 cups water
1/4 cup shelled pistachio nuts, roughly chopped
1/2 cup currants

For the soup: Combine the split peas and vegetable stock in a large saucepan. Bring to a boil, turn down the heat, and simmer briskly for 15 minutes. While the peas are cooking, combine 3/4 teaspoon of the powdered harissa spices with the garlic, mashing it thoroughly with a knife. Set aside in a small bowl. Add the turnips and onions to the stock and cook 15 minutes more. Stir in the garlic and harissa mixture and the mustard greens. Lay the rosemary on the top and cover to keep warm.

For the MEV: Bring the water to a boil; stir in the remaining harissa, couscous, and salt. Remove from the heat and let it stand for 5 minutes. Fluff the couscous with a fork and add the pistachios and currants. Fill 4 MEV or other 1-cup molds with the couscous mixture and press down hard.

To serve: Remove the couscous from the molds and set in the middle of 4 hot soup bowls. Discard the rosemary sprig and ladle the soup around the couscous. Dust with just a little more harissa.

Time Estimate: Preparation, 15 minutes; cooking, 5 minutes; unsupervised, 30 minutes

Nutritional Profile per Serving: Calories—498; % calories from fat—13%; fat (gm)—7 or 11% daily value; saturated fat (gm)—1; sodium (mg)—346; cholesterol (mg)—0; carbohydrates (gm)—85; dietary fiber (gm)—11; protein (gm)—29

Ostrich Neck Soup with Vegetables and Mushrooms

This delicious soup is based on a classic stock made from a not–so–classic meat. Please turn to page 84 for a full discussion of ostrich. The soup can also be prepared with oxtails.

Serves 4

Stock or sauce base

2 pounds ostrich neck or oxtails, cut into 2-inch (5-cm) sections
1 teaspoon light olive oil with a dash of toasted sesame oil
1 onion, peeled and roughly chopped
3 cloves garlic, peeled, bashed, and chopped
1 carrot, roughly chopped
2 stalks celery, roughly chopped
3 tablespoons low-sodium tomato paste
2 (16-ounce or 454-gm) cans low-sodium beef broth
6 sprigs fresh thyme
1/4 teaspoon salt
1/4 teaspoon freshly ground black pepper
1 cup de-alcoholized red wine

Soup

4 cups water
1/4 cup barley
2 cups peeled and diced carrots
1 cup peeled and diced turnips
1 cup quartered mushrooms

Turn the oven to broil. Rinse the neck pieces and lay them on a rack in a broiler pan. Brown for 15 minutes under the broiler; turn and brown the other side for another 15 minutes. While the meat is browning, heat the oil in a pressure cooker or large saucepan on medium high heat. Fry the onion for 2 minutes; add the garlic and fry for 1 minute more. Drop the carrot and celery in and add the tomato paste. Stir until the tomato paste darkens, then add the beef broth, thyme, salt, and pepper. Add the browned meat; rinse the browning pan with the wine and pour into the stock. Bring to a boil, turn down the heat, and simmer, covered, for 3 hours or until the meat is falling off the bones. If you are using a pressure cooker, bring the pressure up to high, and cook for 30 minutes, and quick-release.

When the stock is ready, pour through a sieve into a fat strainer. Take out the ostrich neck pieces and discard the vegetables. When the ostrich is cool enough to handle, pull the meat from the bones and reserve. Discard the bones. At this point the stock can be used either as a soup base or a sauce base.

To make the soup: Pour the water, barley, and soup base into a large saucepan and bring to a boil. Turn down the heat and simmer for 10 minutes, then add the carrots and turnips and simmer until tender, about 15 more minutes. Tip the mushrooms and reserved meat into the soup and heat through.

To serve: Ladle the hot soup into large bowls and serve with a crusty piece of Rustic French Bread (page 171) on the side.

Time Estimate: Preparation, 20 minutes; cooking, 50 minutes; unsupervised, 3 hours or 30 minutes, depending on which method you use.

Nutritional Profile per Serving (using ostrich): Calories—224; % calories from fat—17%; fat (gm)—4 or 7% daily value; saturated fat (gm)—0; sodium (mg)—280; cholesterol (mg)—49. Analysis includes suggested side dishes.

South American Vegetable Soup

There are some unusual ingredients in this soup, but don't let that stop you. You may substitute any yellow or green summer squash for the chayote or pattypan squashes. Our old friend zucchini would work fine. You will find canned tomatillos in the Mexican section of a well-stocked grocery store or in a Mexican market, if you can't get them fresh. The chipotle sauce provides a distinctive smoky flavor that's not to be missed.

Serves 4

- 1/2 teaspoon light olive oil with a dash of toasted sesame oil
- 1/2 onion, peeled and roughly diced
- 1 large clove garlic, bashed, peeled, and chopped
- 1 teaspoon oregano
- 1/4 teaspoon ground allspice
- 1/2 teaspoon ground cumin
- 2 medium thin-skinned potatoes (such as Yukon Gold), peeled and roughly diced
- 4 cups low-sodium vegetable stock (see page 210)
- 4 fresh tomatillos, husks removed and cut into eighths (1/2 cup), or drained canned tomatillos
- 1 (14½-ounce or 411-gm) can no-salt tomatoes, diced in juice
- 1 cup canned black beans, rinsed and drained
- 1/2 cup frozen corn kernels
- 1 chayote squash, peeled, cored, and roughly diced
- 1 pattypan squash, roughly diced
- 1/2 teaspoon chipotle sauce
- 1/4 teaspoon salt

Garnish
2 tablespoons chopped fresh cilantro

Heat the oil in a large saucepan over medium high heat and fry the onion until it becomes translucent, about 2 minutes. Toss in the garlic, oregano, allspice, cumin, and potatoes and cook another 3 minutes, stirring so the garlic doesn't brown. Pour a little of the stock into the pan to release the flavorful bits that might have stuck there. Stir in the rest of the stock, the tomatillos, and tomatoes. Bring to boil, turn the heat down, and allow it to simmer briskly for 15 minutes, or until the potatoes are tender. Add the beans, corn, cactus, squash, chipotle sauce, and salt. Bring back to a boil, turn down the heat, and simmer for 5 minutes,

To serve: Ladle into bowls and sprinkle cilantro on top.

Time Estimate: Preparation, 20 minutes; cooking, 35 minutes

Nutritional Profile per Serving: Calories—205; % calories from fat—7%; fat (gm)—2 or 3% daily value; saturated fat (gm)—0; sodium (mg)—345; cholesterol (mg)—0; carbohydrates (gm)—43; dietary fiber (gm)—9; protein (gm)—12

The Pressure Cooker

I like equipment that saves real time on the longer tasks such as steaming puddings, braising meats, and, of course, cooking beans and whole grains in all their wonderful varieties. But it must also deliver good flavor and preserve nutrients.

The new pressure cookers do this through using less water by restricting the amount of vapor that is released under pressure. Second-generation units have multiple vent holes and two additional fail-safe blowout valves. In the case of the Swiss-made Kuhn Rikon unit, a visual double red band on a stem rises according to pressure and directs you to turn down the heat a notch.

All of this means better safety and less water necessary. Sometimes you need as little as 1/4 cup, which is exceptional news for water-soluble vitamins and retained flavor molecules. There is absolutely no question about it—you'll save time and get better finished food.

Modern pressure cookers come in all shapes and sizes. My preference is the 5 liter. It holds 5¼ quarts and can cook a 3½-pound stewing chicken. It can also make enough beans in one session for several meals.

Pressure Cooker

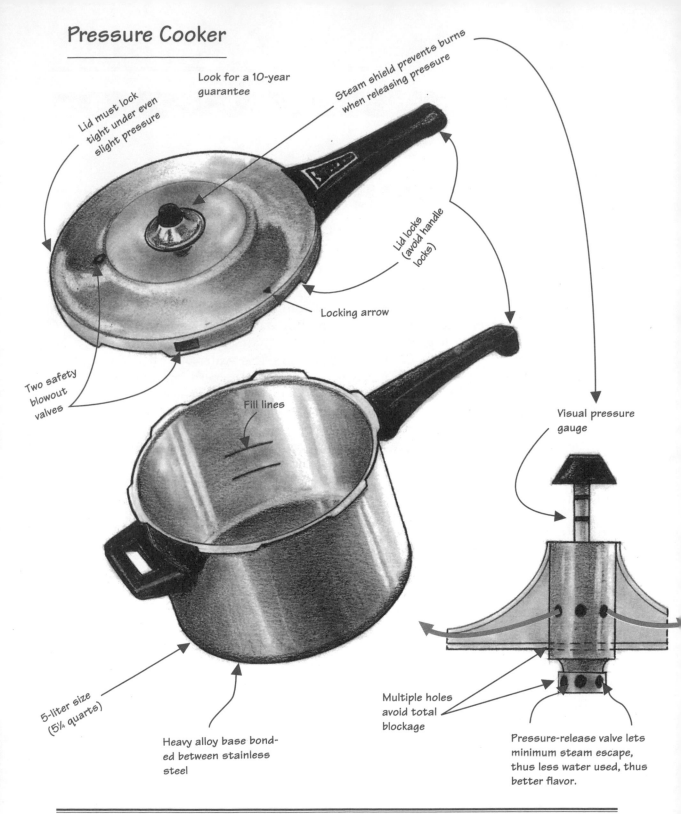

Lid must lock tight under even slight pressure

Look for a 10-year guarantee

Steam shield prevents burns when releasing pressure

Lid locks (avoid handle locks)

Locking arrow

Two safety blowout valves

Visual pressure gauge

Fill lines

5-liter size (5¼ quarts)

Heavy alloy base bonded between stainless steel

Multiple holes avoid total blockage

Pressure-release valve lets minimum steam escape, thus less water used, thus better flavor.

German-Style Vegetable Soup with Franks

Serves 6

1 teaspoon light olive oil with a dash of toasted sesame oil
1 onion, cut in quarters and sliced
2 cloves garlic, peeled, bashed, and chopped
2 carrots, peeled and sliced
2 parsnips, peeled and sliced
2 turnips, quartered and sliced
2 stalks celery, sliced
4 medium Yukon Gold potatoes, peeled, halved, and sliced
1 (14½-ounce or 411-gm) can low-salt tomatoes, diced with juice
6 low- or no-fat franks, cut into 1/2-inch (1.75-cm) slices
1 cup small pasta shells
1/2 teaspoon salt
1/2 teaspoon freshly ground black pepper
2 tablespoons Germany Ethmix (page 217)
4 cups boiling water
3 tablespoons German mustard

Garnish
2 tablespoons chopped fresh parsley

> If hypertension is a problem for you, I suggest you reduce the number of franks or check the package nutrient information to reduce the sodium amount in this recipe.

Preheat the pressure cooker (or a heavy saucepan) and add the oil. Drop in the onions and cook until they wilt, 2 minutes. Add the garlic, carrots, parsnips, turnips, celery, and potatoes and cook for 2 minutes. Stir in the tomatoes, franks, pasta, salt, pepper, and spice mix. Pour in the water, cover, and bring the pressure up on high heat, which will take about 10 minutes. Reduce the heat to medium and cook for 4 minutes at high pressure. Remove from the heat and release the pressure by running cold water over the top. (Simmer covered for 1 hour over very low heat if you are not using a pressure cooker.) Remove the cover and stir in the mustard. If you do not have a pressure cooker, simply simmer the soup in a saucepan for 45 minutes before adding the mustard.

To serve: Ladle into bowls, and sprinkle chopped parsley on top. Offer Hearty Whole Wheat Quinoa Bread (page 173) in a napkin-lined basket.

Time Estimate: Preparation, 20 minutes; cooking, 20 minutes; unsupervised, 1 hour (without pressure cooker)

Nutritional Profile per Serving: Calories—364; % calories from fat—7%; fat (gm)—3 or 4% daily value; saturated fat (gm)—0; sodium (mg)—873; cholesterol (mg)—15; carbohydrates (gm)—70; dietary fiber (gm)—8; protein (gm)—15. Analysis includes suggested side dishes.

Bean Soup with Sausage and Mushrooms

My local rural grocery store began carrying prepared polenta last summer. It looks like a yellow salami wrapped in plastic which you can slice right through. It is convenient, tasty, and low in fat and sodium. A good product for the swift refrigerator. It's made by San Gennaro Foods Inc., which can be reached at 1–800–462–1916 for information on where to get it in your area.

Serves 4

1/4 cup dried Great Northern beans
1/4 cup dried red kidney beans
1/4 cup dried pinto beans
1 tablespoon light olive oil with a dash of toasted sesame oil
2 medium onions, sliced
1/4 teaspoon summer savory
1/4 teaspoon chili powder
2 cups low-sodium chicken stock (page 207), heated to boiling
8 ounces (227 gm) prepared polenta, cut into 4 slices
6 ounces (170 gm) smoked low-fat turkey sausage, sliced on the diagonal into 1/4-inch (.75-cm) pieces
6 medium mushrooms, cut into quarters
1/3 cup de-alcoholized red wine
2 large collard green leaves, cut into 1/4-inch (.75-cm) strips, 1 inch (2.5 cm) long
1/3 cup roughly chopped roasted red bell pepper
1/16 teaspoon freshly ground black pepper
1 tablespoon arrowroot mixed with 2 tablespoons de-alcoholized red wine (slurry)

> I use a whole tablespoon of oil in this recipe to ensure that the foam from the cooking beans doesn't plug the pressure cooker vents. If you want to cook this dish the long way, you may use 1 teaspoon of oil to fry the onions, then cook the soaked beans for 2 hours. When the beans are tender, follow the rest of the recipe as written.

Combine the beans and soak them overnight, or quick–soak by covering with cold water, bringing to a boil, and soaking for 1 hour.

Heat the oil in the pressure cooker and cook the onions over high heat, stirring, until translucent, about 1 or 2 minutes. Add the soaked beans, savory, and chili powder and mix. Pour in the hot chicken broth, secure the lid, and bring the pressure up over high heat. When the pressure cooker reaches full pressure, turn the heat down to low and start the timer. Cook at full pressure for 9 minutes.

While the beans are cooking, lay the polenta slices on a platform in a Stack and Steam or other large steamer. Cover and heat over gently boiling water for 8 minutes.

Release the pressure immediately by running cold water over the top of the pressure cooker. Remove the top, set the pressure cooker over medium high heat, and bring to a boil. Stir in the sausage slices, mushrooms, and wine and simmer for 2 minutes. Stir the collard strips, red bell pepper, and ground black pepper into the bean mixture and cook for 4 minutes. Remove from the heat, stir in the arrowroot slurry, and cook until thickened.

To serve: The soup may be served in a large bowl over the top of a polenta slice. Serve with the lovely dark green Steamed Collard Greens (page 153).

Time Estimate: Preparation, 20 minutes; cooking, 15 minutes; unsupervised, overnight or 1 hour, depending on method

Variation: To make this super-swift, try using 1/2 cup each canned low-sodium Great Northern, kidney, and pinto beans. Cook the onion in the oil, add the beans, stock, and the rest of the ingredients, and simmer 10 minutes to allow the flavors to marry. Thicken and serve as indicated above.

Unused canned beans combine well in salads and soups if used within 2 to 3 days.

Nutritional Profile per Serving: Calories—381; % calories from fat—14%; fat (gm)—6 or 9% daily value; saturated fat (gm)—1; sodium (mg)—535; cholesterol (mg)—19; carbohydrates (gm) 66; dietary fiber (gm)—15; protein (gm)—20

Asian Sunflower Sprout and Red Pepper Salad

Serves 4

1 large sweet red bell pepper
1 tablespoon rice wine vinegar
1 teaspoon low-sodium tamari
1/4 teaspoon toasted sesame oil
1/8 teaspoon Shanghai Coastline Ethmix (page 215)
4 cups sunflower seed sprouts

Bring water to a boil in the bottom of a Stack and Steam or other large steamer. Cut the red pepper in half lengthwise and trim off the stem, removing the seeds and veins. Cut the pepper into long, slender strips. Steam the strips for 4 minutes. Remove and set aside to cool.

In a small bowl, whisk together the vinegar, tamari, sesame oil, and spice mix. Toss with the sunflower sprouts and steamed red pepper strips to coat thoroughly.

Nutritional Profile per Serving: Calories—91; % calories from fat—7%; fat (gm)—less than 1 or 1% daily value; saturated fat (gm)—0; sodium (mg)—67; cholesterol (mg)—0; carbohydrates (gm)—18; dietary fiber (gm)—3; protein (gm)—7

Butter Lettuce and Arugula Salad

Serves 4

Honey Mustard Dressing
1/4 cup dressing base (see page 213)
1/2 teaspoon Dijon mustard
1/8 teaspoon honey
1/8 teaspoon freshly ground black pepper

Salad
4 cups butter lettuce leaves
1 cup arugula or watercress
4 Roma tomatoes

Combine the dressing ingredients and set aside. Wash and spin-dry the lettuce and arugula. Cut the tomatoes into 8 wedges each. Place the vegetables in a salad bowl, drizzle the dressing over the top, and toss.

Nutritional Profile per Serving: Calories—29; % calories from fat—13%; fat (gm)—less than 1 or 1% daily value; saturated fat (gm)—0; sodium (mg)—28; cholesterol (mg)—0; carbohydrates (gm)—6; dietary fiber (gm)—1; protein (gm)—1

Papaya Salad

Serves 4

    2 cups cubed papaya
    1/2 cup chopped jicama
    1 teaspoon finely chopped mint
    3 tablespoons lime juice
    1/8 teaspoon ground allspice

Toss the papaya, jicama, mint, and lime juice together in a mixing bowl and sprinkle with the allspice. Stir to mix well.

Nutritional Profile per Serving: Calories—36; % calories from fat—3%; fat (gm)—less than 1 or 1% daily value; saturated fat (gm)—0; sodium (mg)—3; cholesterol (mg)—0; carbohydrates (gm)—9; dietary fiber (gm)—2; protein (gm)—0

Cucumber and Apple Salad

Serves 4

    8 butter lettuce leaves
    1 small English cucumber, peeled, seeded, and chopped
    1 small tart apple, quartered, cored, thinly sliced, and chopped
    1/2 cup nonfat plain yogurt
    1/2 teaspoon chopped fresh mint leaves
    1/16 teaspooon ground red pepper (cayenne)
    1/8 teaspoon salt

Lay 2 lettuce leaves on each of 4 plates. Combine the cucumber and apple in a medium bowl and scoop onto the lettuce leaves. Whisk together the yogurt, mint, cayenne, and salt in a small mixing bowl. Top the cucumber and apples with a dollop of yogurt dressing.

Nutritional Profile per Serving: Calories—54; % calories from fat—3%; fat (gm)—less than 1 or 1% daily value; saturated fat (gm)—0; sodium (mg)—93; cholesterol (mg)—0; carbohydrates (gm)—11; dietary fiber (gm)—2; protein (gm)—3

Cantaloupe Salad

Serves 4

1/4 teaspoon ground ginger
2 tablespoons freshly squeezed lime juice
1 cantaloupe, peeled and seeds removed, sliced into thin strips

Stir the ground ginger into the lime juice and pour over the cantaloupe strips in a bowl. Let stand a few minutes before serving.

Nutritional Profile per Serving: Calories—50; % calories from fat—7%; fat (gm)—less than 1 or 1% daily value; saturated fat (gm)—0; sodium (mg)—12; cholesterol (mg)—0; carbohydrates (gm)—12; dietary fiber (gm)—1; protein (gm)—1

Black Bean Salsa

Serves 4

1/2 cup sliced green onions (about 3 onions)
1/2 cup frozen corn kernels
1/2 cup canned black beans, rinsed and drained
1 cup chopped tomatoes
2 tablespoons chopped pickled jalapeños
15 cilantro leaves, chopped
2 tablespoons freshly squeezed lime juice
1/2 teaspoon ground cumin
1/4 teaspoon salt

Combine all the ingredients in a bowl and toss to mix. Serve with White Bean and Green Chili Quesadillas (page 50).

Nutritional Profile per Serving: Calories—62; % calories from fat—0%; fat (gm)—0 or 0% daily value; saturated fat (gm)—0; sodium (mg)—236; cholesterol (mg)—0; carbohydrates (gm)—13; dietary fiber (gm)—3; protein (gm)—3

Mexican Cucumber

Serves 4

2 English (hot house) cucumbers, peeled and cut in half crosswise
1/4 cup freshly squeezed lime juice
1/2 teaspoon Shanghai Coastline Ethmix (page 215)

Cut each cucumber piece lengthwise down to the last inch (2.5 cm). Make another lengthwise cut across the first, resulting in 4 long pieces held together at the bottom by that last inch. Mix the spices with the lime juice in a medium bowl. Dip the cucumbers in the liquid to coat the cut quarters. Chill in the refrigerator or on a bed of ice for at least an hour before serving.

To serve: Double an 18-inch (45-cm) length of waxed paper and fold it into a triangle. Roll the cucumber into the waxed paper, uncut end down, with about 3 inches (7.5 cm) exposed. Push the cucumber up from the bottom to eat.

Nutritional Profile per Serving: Calories—24; % calories from fat—8%; fat (gm)—less than 1 or 1% daily value; saturated fat (gm)—0; sodium (mg)—3; cholesterol (mg)—0; carbohydrates (gm)—6; dietary fiber (gm)—1; protein (gm)—1

Breakfast and Lunch Dishes

The Omelet and the Pan

once again the omelet is voted world's most popular swift food

The omelet is perhaps the world's most popular swift food. The simplest omelets are made of eggs and butter, but it rarely stops there. We often add cream and rich garnishes such as cheeses, caviar, and sour cream. The chart shows what can happen to the nutritional numbers as we elaborate on the basic recipe. The final set of numbers is for an omelet in which we use egg substitute, nonfat cheese, and a tiny amount of butter—and what a difference it makes! (See page 35 for a recipe that makes up for the reduced fat, calories, and cholesterol with lots of vivid spicings and flavors.)

	Calories	Fat gm.	Sat. Fat gm.	% of Cals. from Fat	Sodium gm.
3 eggs + 1 Tblsp. butter	325	27	12	73%	543
3 eggs + 6 Tblsp. cream	587	54	29	83%	573
3 eggs + 6 Tblsp. cream + 3 oz. Brie + 1/2 oz. caviar + 2 oz. sour cream	989	88	50	80%	1524
Egg substitute (whites) + 1 oz. nonfat Swiss cheese + 1/4 tsp. butter	107	1	1	10%	631

The classic omelet pan doubles as a French crêpe pan. It is very flat and shallow, with sloping sides and a depth of a mere inch, traditionally made of cast iron with metal handles. In the contemporary version, the original seven-inch pan shape curled its sides and was deepened to hold three eggs. Eventually a nonstick version was developed but the shape remained essentially the same.

An alternative design to the traditional French omelet pan, influenced by the aesthetics of Asia, is oblong with a handle and a perfectly flat, nonstick surface. One end is sloped to ease transfer from pan to plate. This version has been used to great effect in "Treena's Square Eggs" (page 33) and other recipes in the following pages.

Treena's Square Eggs

Serves 1

    Olive oil cooking spray
    1/3 cup egg substitute
    1/2 ounce (14 gm) nonfat Swiss cheese
    1/4 teaspoon chipotle sauce
    1/8 teaspoon freshly ground black pepper
    1 teaspoon soy "bacon" bits
    1 teaspoon chopped fresh parsley

Spray the special omelet pan with olive oil cooking spray and place over medium high heat. Pour the egg substitute evenly over the bottom of the hot pan and shake gently to make sure it doesn't stick. When bubbles start to appear on the top of the egg, drop the slice of cheese in the middle. Sprinkle chipotle sauce and pepper over the whole thing. When the cheese just begins to melt, fold each end of the omelet over the center, making a square. The residual heat will finish cooking the top of the eggs and melt the cheese.

Sprinkle the "bacon" bits and parsley on top and serve.

Time Estimate: Hands-on, 5 minutes; cooking, 5 minutes

Nutritional Profile per Serving: Calories—127; % calories from fat—7%; fat (gm)—1 or 1% daily value; saturated fat (gm)—474; cholesterol (mg)—3; carbohydrates (gm)—5; dietary fiber (gm)—0; protein (gm)—23

Treena's square breakfast

Shrimp and Rice Frittata

Serves 4

1 cup cooked and shelled baby shrimp
12 medium black olives, pitted and roughly chopped
1 tablespoon chopped fresh parsley
1/2 cup cooked long-grain white rice (page 163)
1/4 teaspoon ground red pepper (cayenne)
3/8 teaspoon salt, divided
2 teaspoons butter
1/8 teaspoon freshly ground white pepper
1/4 teaspoon dried tarragon
2 cups egg substitute (I prefer Egg Beaters)
4 teaspoons freshly grated Parmesan cheese
1 tablespoon freshly squeezed lemon juice

Bring water to a boil in the bottom of a large steamer.

In a medium heatproof mixing bowl, stir together the shrimp, olives, parsley, rice, cayenne, and 1/4 teaspoon of the salt. Place the bowl in the steamer to heat through for about 3 minutes.

Melt the butter in an omelet pan or other pan with rounded sides over medium high heat. Sprinkle the remaining 1/8 teaspoon of salt and the freshly ground white pepper and tarragon into the egg substitute in a mixing bowl and stir with a fork. Pour into the pan, shaking and stirring with a fork. Once the egg is cooked enough so that little air bubbles start to come up from the base (about 2 minutes), spread the heated shrimp mixture over the top and press down into the omelet. Sprinkle the Parmesan cheese over the top and shake the pan. Continue to cook, moving the pan occasionally to keep the eggs from burning, for a total of 8 minutes.

To serve: Cut the omelet into quarters, place each onto a hot plate, and sprinkle with the lemon juice. Arrange Steamed Asparagus spears (page 150) alongside and serve with Cucumber and Apple Salad (page 25). Complete the plate with a slice of homemade rye bread (page 172).

Time Estimate: Preparation, 15 minutes; cooking, 14 minutes

Nutritional Profile per Serving: Calories—333; % calories from fat—17%; fat (gm)—6 or 10% daily value; saturated fat (gm)—2; sodium (gm)—604; cholesterol (mg)—90; carbohydrates (gm)—41; dietary fiber (gm)—6; protein (gm)—30. Analysis includes suggested side dishes.

Japanese Rolled Omelet

In Japan the beaten eggs are cooked in a rectangular pan, rolled around various fillings, and turned out onto a small bamboo mat. The omelet is gently squeezed into a perfect cylinder, then sliced into 2-inch rounds. Don't let this put you off. You can achieve a delicious result with your old round pan. However, if you treat cooking as a hobby as well as a necessity, I think you'll love this new way of serving a familiar favorite. It's actually a lot of fun.

Flat non-stick interior

Serves 4

Enameled exterior

2 large red bell peppers
1 bunch spinach, washed and stemmed
1/8 teaspoon salt
1/16 teaspoon freshly ground black pepper
1/4 teaspoon grated nutmeg
1/2 teaspoon light olive oil with a dash of toasted sesame oil
2 cups egg substitute (I prefer Egg Beaters)
1/4 cup de-alcoholized Chardonnay wine
2 tablespoons low-sodium tamari

Sloped End

Cut the tops and bottoms off the peppers; remove and discard the cores and seeds, and halve the peppers lengthwise. Place the pepper halves and trimmings on a steamer rack or platform. Bring water to a boil in the bottom of a Stack and Steam or other large steamer. Steam the pepper halves over medium high heat for 20 minutes or until the skin is wrinkled and loose. Remove them and, when cool enough to handle, pull off the loose skin and cut into strips. Reserve 1/2 cup for the sauce.

To cook the spinach: Place the spinach leaves on a platform in the steamer and sprinkle with the salt, pepper, and nutmeg. Steam over medium high heat for 1½ minutes or until the leaves are flat. Remove the spinach from the steamer and press out the juice with a fork.

Without the rectangular pan, over a much lower heat, you can use a small, nonstick square or rectangular baking pan and gently set the egg before rolling. Otherwise, use a regular omelet pan and put up with the irregular ends!

To make the omelet: Preheat a 7 × 5-inch (18 × 12-cm) rectangular Japanese omelet pan over medium low heat and wipe the bottom lightly with oil. Pour 1/3 cup of the eggs in the pan, fully coating the bottom. When the eggs are half-set, lay the pieces of pepper across the middle of the pan and, using chopsticks or a spatula, fold the egg around the pepper away from you so that it rolls up. Now slide the omelet to the end farthest from the handle and turn it out onto the bamboo mat. Pour in another 1/3 cup of eggs. When the eggs are half-set, lay the cooked spinach across the surface and roll up as before. Continue with the remaining egg rolled in the same fashion. Wrap the bamboo mat around the omelet leaving a 1-inch (2.5-cm) overlap. Pull the overlap in tight to squeeze the liquid out of the omelet and to press it into a roll which can be set aside for reheating and slicing. Continue with the remaining egg, half rolled around the spinach, the other half rolled around the red pepper. You will end up with 6 rolls.

To make the sauce: Put the reserved steamed red pepper trimmings, the wine, and the tamari into a blender and whiz until smooth. Press the sauce through a strainer into a bowl.

To serve: Remove the warmed omelet rolls from the steamer. Slice each one into 4 even pieces. Pour a puddle of warm sauce onto each of 4 warmed plates and set 6 pieces of omelet, three with spinach and the others with red peppers, cut side up, on top of the sauce. Offer Cucumber and Apple Salad (page 25) in a small bowl. Serve with Steamed Asparagus spears (page 150) cut diagonally in 1-inch (2.5-cm) pieces alongside the omelet and a bowl of Steamed Pearl Rice (page 163).

Bamboo mat

Rolled eggs

Time Estimate: Preparation, 20 minutes; cooking, 31 minutes

Nutritional Profile per Serving: Calories—287; % calories from fat—4%; fat (gm)—1 or 2% daily value; saturated fat (gm)—0; sodium (mg)—716; cholesterol (mg)—1; carbohydrates (gm)—48; dietary fiber (gm)—4; protein (gm)—20. Analysis includes suggested side dishes.

The Waffle Iron with "Speed Grill" Options

I have made waffles from time to time, but inevitably I found that the electric-powered unit took up too much space on the counter and ended up in the garage—a way station to the rummage sale or the garbage. Then came a new favorite: the classic waffle iron updated with "speed grill" options. This well-thought-out unit can be equipped with inserts that utilize the common source of heat to broil, grill, and toast to make sandwiches or even crisp ice cream wafer biscuits and . . . waffles!

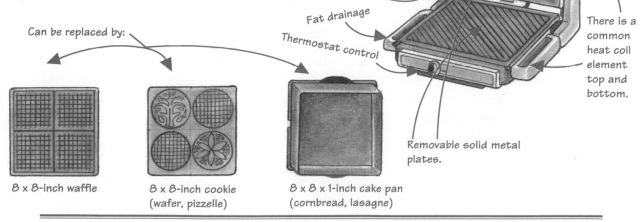

Plates can be reversed for plain griddle-cakes, etc.

Flexible distance hinge allows for food up to 1½ inches thick.

Fat drainage

Thermostat control

There is a common heat coil element top and bottom.

Removable solid metal plates.

Can be replaced by:

8 x 8-inch waffle

8 x 8-inch cookie (wafer, pizzelle)

8 x 8 x 1-inch cake pan (cornbread, lasagne)

Savory Waffles

Serves 4

1¾ cups all-purpose flour
1 tablespoon baking powder
2 cups nonfat milk
1/4 cup egg substitute
1 tablespoon light olive oil with a dash of toasted sesame oil
1 cup grated nonfat Swiss cheese
4 thin slices Canadian bacon, chopped (2 ounces or 57 gm)
1/4 teaspoon freshly ground black pepper

Garnish
1 tablespoon freshly grated Parmesan cheese
1 tablespoon chopped chives
1 tablespoon individual chive flowers (optional)

Preheat the waffle iron for 10 minutes or until the indicator light goes out. Preheat the oven to 200°F (100°C). Combine the flour and baking powder and whisk together in a large bowl. Whisk the milk, egg substitute, and oil together in a separate bowl and pour into the dry ingredients. Stir until well mixed and smooth. Gently stir in the Swiss cheese, Canadian bacon, and black pepper.

Brush the preheated waffle iron lightly with oil. Pour in approximately 1/2 cup of batter per waffle square, or enough to cover the entire iron. Bake until the steam stops or the indicator light goes out, 5 to 8 minutes. Lay the finished waffles on racks in the oven to keep warm while you bake the rest.

To serve: Dust each hot waffle with Parmesan cheese and scatter chives and chive flowers over the top. Serve with the Papaya Salad (page 25).

Time Estimate: Preparation, 15 minutes; unsupervised, 20 minutes or longer depending on the size of your waffle iron

Nutritional Profile per Serving: Calories—355; % calories from fat—14%; fat (gm)—5 or 8% daily value; saturated fat (gm)— 1; sodium (mg)—696; cholesterol (mg)—12; carbohydrates (gm)—56; dietary fiber (gm)—3; protein (gm)—20. Analysis includes suggested side dishes.

Balinese Potato Waffles

Serves 4

1¾ cups sifted all-purpose flour

1½ teaspoons Bali Ethmix (see recipe page 218)

1 tablespoon baking powder

1/4 teaspoon salt

1/4 cup egg substitute

2 cups nonfat milk

1 tablespoon light olive oil with a dash of toasted sesame oil

2 medium russet potatoes, peeled, boiled for 10 minutes, and grated (3 cups)

2 tablespoons chopped fresh parsley

1/4 teaspoon freshly ground black pepper

1 cup sweetened applesauce

4 tablespoons yogurt cheese (see page 210)

Preheat the waffle iron while you make the batter. Preheat the oven to 200°F (100°C). Sift the flour, the homemade or purchased seasoning mix, the baking powder, and the salt together into a large mixing bowl. Combine the egg substitute, milk, and oil in a smaller bowl. Pour the wet ingredients into the dry ingredients and mix with an electric mixer or by hand until the batter is smooth. Stir in the grated potatoes, parsley, and black pepper.

Lightly coat the preheated waffle iron with vegetable oil cooking spray and pour in about 1/2 cup of batter per square, or enough to just cover the entire iron. Bake until the steam stops or the indicator light goes out, 5 to 8 minutes. Lay the finished waffles on racks in the oven to keep warm while you bake the rest.

Serve on heated plates with a spoonful of applesauce and a dollop of yogurt cheese. Offer Papaya Salad (see page 25) on the side.

Time Estimate: Preparation, 15 minutes; cooking, 10 minutes; unsupervised, 20 to 32 minutes

Nutritional Profile per Serving: Calories—441; % calories from fat—9%; fat (gm)—5 or 7% daily value; saturated fat (gm)—0; sodium (mg)—394; cholesterol (mg)—3; carbohydrates (gm)—87; dietary fiber (gm)—5; protein (gm)—15. Analysis includes suggested side dishes.

The Multiple-Duty Indoor Compression Grill

I'm very fond of this piece of equipment because it appeals to my sense of logic. Why not equip a toaster-sized plug-in grill with cooking surfaces that are easily removed and replaced by other metal surfaces that perform other tasks?

The model that I prefer, and the one used in the accompanying illustrations, is the Toastmaster Speed Grill. It serves as a waffle iron, open griddle, open grill, top and bottom grill, and pizzelle iron, and it can be used to bake with a special 8-inch pan. (I used this model to make the waffles in the previous section of this book, beginning on page 38.)

Basically, the compression grill is a flat toaster with built-in elements that heat removable metal plates. When opened it provides a ribbed or plain 8 × 16-inch surface. The hinged-lid back support allows the top surface to lay flat on foods up to 1½ inches thick.

My favorite use, and the one that justifies its prominent place on my counter (and I don't give up that space easily), is the ribbed or plain-surface compression grill, where the heated surfaces make a "sandwich" out of the food to be cooked and, in so doing, shorten the time by almost half. An inch-thick halibut steak is ready in about 4 minutes and is extraordinarily moist and succulent. The moisture retention exceeds that of radiant pan broiling or a simple sauté.

The only drawback for a larger family is its size. The grill is perfect for two and a real pinch for four, but then I'd be loath to have it on display if it were any bigger.

Compression Grill

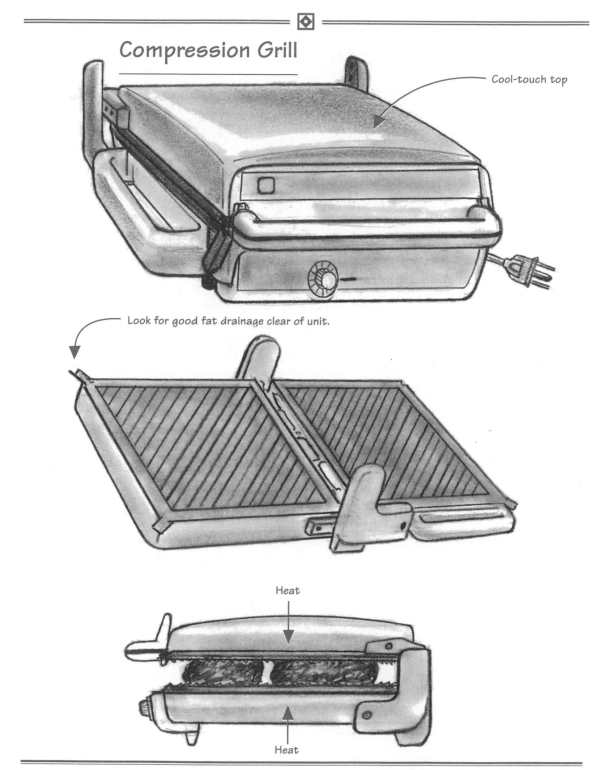

Cool-touch top

Look for good fat drainage clear of unit.

Heat

Heat

Panini with Prosciutto and Fennel

Serves 6

3 small fennel bulbs, trimmed and sliced lengthwise into 1/4-inch (6 cm) pieces
1 recipe Focaccia (page 170)
4 ounces (113 gm) nonfat mozzarella cheese, sliced
4 fresh sage leaves, cut into thin strips (chiffonade)
4 ounces (113 gm) thinly sliced lean prosciutto
1/8 teaspoon freshly ground black pepper
2 teaspoons extra virgin olive oil

Preheat the compression grill for 10 minutes. Steam the fennel slices until tender, about 2 minutes. Spray the grill with vegetable oil cooking spray and grill the large slices of steamed fennel for 1 minute. Remove to a plate and cover with a lid to keep warm.

Cut the focaccia in half, then slice each piece horizontally. Open the bread up on the kitchen counter and lay half the cheese slices on one side of each large sandwich. Scatter a little sage over the cheese, lay on slices of fennel and prosciutto, add the rest of the sage, and dust with freshly ground black pepper. Place the lids on the sandwiches, brush the tops with 1/2 teaspoon of oil, and dust with a little more fresh pepper. Spray the grill again and bake one sandwich at a time for 6 minutes each. Keep the first panino warm while you grill the second.

You can grill these in a heavy skillet lightly coated with cooking spray. Cook them for 3 minutes per side, pressing down when you put them in the pan and again when you turn them. Cut each large sandwich into 6 smaller ones.

To serve: Offer 2 pieces on a plate with the Butter Lettuce and Arugula Salad on page 24.

Time Estimate: Preparation, 15 minutes; cooking, 15 minutes

Nutritional Profile per Serving: Calories—397; % calories from fat—17 %; fat (gm)—8 or 12% daily value; saturated fat (gm)—2; sodium (mg)—568; cholesterol (mg)—20; carbohydrates (gm)—63; dietary fiber (gm)—8; protein (gm)—19. Analysis includes suggested side dishes.

Panini with Peas, Sun-Dried Tomatoes, and Olives

Serves 6

8 sun-dried tomato halves
1/2 cup frozen green peas, thawed
12 kalamata olives, pitted and sliced
1 recipe Focaccia (page 170)
1/8 teaspoon freshly ground black pepper, divided
20 leaves fresh oregano
4 ounces (113 gm) nonfat mozzarella cheese, sliced
2 teaspoons extra-virgin olive oil

Bring the tomatoes to a boil in water to cover in a small saucepan. Remove from the heat and let them soak for 10 minutes. Drain and slice. Mash the peas with a fork and stir in the tomatoes and olives. Preheat the compression grill on high for 10 minutes.

Cut the focaccia in 4 pieces, then slice each piece horizontally. Open the bread on the kitchen counter and spread the pea mixture on the bottom halves of the 4 sandwiches; sprinkle with freshly ground black pepper. Scatter on fresh oregano leaves and top each with a slice of cheese. Close the sandwiches with the top halves of the focaccia and brush each with 1/2 teaspoon of the oil. Dust the top with freshly ground black pepper and bake for 5 or 6 minutes in the preheated grill. Without the compression grill, these may be pan-broiled in a heavy skillet for 2 or 3 minutes per side, pressing down on the sandwiches when you lay them in the pan and again when you turn them.

To serve: Cut each sandwich in half diagonally and serve on a plate with the Butter Lettuce and Arugula salad (page 24).

Time Estimate: Preparation, 10 minutes; cooking, 16 minutes

Nutritional Profile per Serving: Calories—355; % calories from fat—18%; fat (gm)—7 or 11% daily value; saturated fat (gm)—0; sodium (mg)—387; cholesterol (mg)—3; carbohydrates (gm)—58; dietary fiber (gm)—5; protein (gm)—15. Analysis includes suggested side dishes.

Canadian Bacon, Roasted Peppers, and Cheese on a Muffin

Serves 4

4 English muffins, sliced in half
4 very thin slices Canadian bacon
1 teaspoon Dijon mustard
1/2 cup canned roasted red pepper slices
1/16 teaspoon freshly ground black pepper
4 large basil leaves
4 (1-ounce) slices nonfat Swiss cheese

Preheat the compression grill on high heat. To ensure a good texture, toast the insides of the English muffins by reversing the halves and grilling for 1 minute. Lay the muffins, toasted side up, on the kitchen counter and place a slice of Canadian bacon on the bottom half of each. Spread 1/4 teaspoon mustard on each slice of bacon and cover with 1/8 cup red pepper strips. Sprinkle with freshly ground black pepper. Add a basil leaf, a slice of cheese, and the top of the English muffin and grill for 4 minutes.

Serve with Mexican Cucumber (page 27).

Time Estimate: Preparation, 10 minutes; cooking, 4 minutes

Nutritional Profile per Serving: Calories—214; % calories from fat—7%; fat (gm)—2 or 3% daily value; saturated fat (gm)—0; sodium (mg)—702; cholesterol (mg)—7; carbohydrates (gm)—35; dietary fiber (gm)—3; protein (gm)—15. Analysis includes suggested side dishes.

Smoked Salmon and White Beans in Pita Bread

Serves 4

1/4 teaspoon dried summer savory
1/8 teaspoon freshly ground black pepper
1/2 cup canned white beans, rinsed, drained, and mashed
8 ounces smoked salmon, shredded (about 1 cup)
1/2 cup yogurt cheese (page 210)
1 teaspoon prepared horseradish
1 tablespoon chopped fresh parsley
2 teaspoons freshly squeezed lemon juice
2 whole wheat pita breads, cut in half crosswise to make 4 pockets

Preheat the compression grill on high heat. Stir the savory and pepper into the mashed beans. Add the salmon, yogurt cheese, horseradish, parsley, and lemon juice. Stir with a fork until thoroughly mixed. Divide mixture among the 4 pita halves. Grill the filled pitas for 4 minutes and remove to a warm plate. Without a compression grill, simply oven-broil or pan-broil for 3 or 4 minutes on either side. Spoon some Mexican Cucumber (page 27) onto the plate and enjoy!

Time Estimate: Preparation, 15 minutes; cooking, 3 minutes

Nutritional Profile per Serving: Calories—218; % calories from fat—15%; fat (gm)—4 or 5% daily value; saturated fat (gm)—0; sodium (mg)—616; cholesterol (mg)—14; carbohydrates (gm)—29; dietary fiber (gm)—5; protein (gm)—19. Analysis includes suggested side dishes.

Canned Beans

Now let me introduce you to the *swift bean*. I've got pinto for Mexican dishes, adzuki for Asian, garbanzo for Middle Eastern, black for South American, kidney for Caribbean, navy for New England, and Great Northern as a personal favorite for the Pacific Northwest and some Italian dishes. They are already prepared in a can from certified organic farms with a special combination of potassium and sodium that keeps flavor high and risk low—which means that I'm now able to keep a full range of beans in my pantry. Price and flavor absorption are the only reasons I can offer in support of cooking your own.

	SOAK	SIMMER (Hours)	PRESSURE COOKED (Minutes)	$ RAW*	$ CANNED	MAX SAVINGS PER LB
PINTO 15 OZ.	YES	1.5 to 2	4 to 6	.34	1.45	1.11
ADZUKI 15 OZ.	YES	1.5 to 2	5 to 9	.49	1.45	.96
GARBANZO 15 OZ.	YES	2 to 3	13 to 17	.45	1.45	1.00
BLACK 15 OZ.	YES	1.5	5 to 9	.40	1.45	1.05
KIDNEY 15 OZ.	YES	1.5 to 2	10 to 12	.53	1.45	.92
NAVY 15 OZ.	YES	1.5 to 2	6 to 8	.53	1.45	.92
GREAT NORTHERN 24 OZ.	YES	1.5 to 2	4 to 8	.40	1.45	1.05

* Raw price (dried) is based upon 1 pound packaged weight: .38 of 1 lb. = 1-1/2 cups cooked (the same as solids in a 15-oz. can). Canned values are given from Eden Organic Beans.

Looking at this chart I can see a difference of about 33 cents per 1/2-cup serving per pound, from which I would need to take off the average two-hour energy cost. Then there's my time versus the convenience.

But more than all of this is the *immediate variety* I'm offered for meatless meals that provide adequate protein at a very reasonable price when compared to meat and even poultry.

As a further means of encouragement, could I now offer you a list of those herbs and spices that will enhance your enjoyment of these lower-sodium newcomers? Try summer or winter savory, cumin, Germany or Poland Ethmix (page 217), bay leaves, oregano, parsley, and, for my taste, cilantro when added in small amounts just before serving.

You may also find that the method of processing used by the Eden Foods Company and others will actually reduce the effects of strachynose and rufinos, those gas-producing ruffians feared by us all!

The following chart will help you to determine the benefits of using beans to replace part or all of your meat servings. I've included potatoes and rice to let you compare beans with our traditional starches.

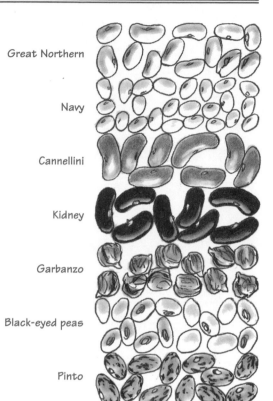

Great Northern

Navy

Cannellini

Kidney

Garbanzo

Black-eyed peas

Pinto

Navy Bean

Serving Size 1/2 cup (115 gm)	Pinto	Adzuki	Garbanzo	Black	Kidney	Navy	Great Northern	Potato	Rice
Calories	117	147	134	113	112	129	104	68	133
Fat	0	0	2	0	0	0.5	0	0	0
Sodium	2	9	6	1	1	1	2	3	1
Potassium	398	612	239	355	335	335	344	262	28
Carbohydrate	22	29	22	20	20	24	19	16	29
Fiber	7	1	4	7	17	8	5	1	1
Protein	7	9	7	8	8	8	7	1	3

Moroccan Chick Peas on Pita

Serves 3

1 teaspoon light olive oil with a dash of toasted sesame oil

1/2 onion, finely chopped

4 cloves garlic, peeled, bashed, and chopped

1/2 cup raisins

2 teaspoons Morocco Ethmix (page 218)

1½ cups canned 50% less salt garbanzo beans,
   rinsed and drained

1 cup no-sodium vegetable stock (page 210)

1 tablespoon freshly squeezed lemon juice

3 whole wheat pitas

Side salad

3 generous sprays of arugula or watercress

2 Roma tomatoes, thinly sliced

1/4 cup yogurt cheese (page 210)

2 tablespoons soft goat cheese (optional)

> The cooking time of chick peas seems to vary a lot—up to 2 hours, in my experience. One way to deal with this is to cook a big potful when you have plenty of time and freeze them in Ziploc bags. Another way is to buy low-sodium canned garbanzos and use them rinsed and drained.

Preheat the compression grill on high for 10 minutes. Heat the oil in a high-sided skillet over medium high heat. Fry the onions for 1 minute just to release the oils, then add the garlic and cook 1 more minute. Add the raisins, spice mix, garbanzo beans, vegetable stock, and lemon juice. Turn the heat to high and boil for 5 minutes to reduce the amount of liquid and plump the raisins. Mash the beans in the pan with a potato masher to break them up and incorporate liquid.

Cut the pitas in half and spread the inside of each with 3 tablespoons of the bean mixture. Fit 3 halves on the hot grill and broil for 4 minutes. Repeat with the other 3 pita halves. Without a compression grill, simply oven-broil or pan-broil for 3 minutes on either side.

To serve: Arrange the arugula or watercress and the tomato slices on each plate and lay 2 pita halves beside them. Combine the yogurt and goat cheese, if you decide to use it, and place a dollop alongside. (The goat cheese will add 28 calories and 2 grams of fat.) To eat on the run, open the pita half and insert the arugula, tomato slices, and yogurt inside.

Time Estimate: Preparation, 10 minutes; cooking, 7 minutes; unsupervised, 8 minutes

Nutritional Profile per Serving: Calories—432; % calories from fat—11%; fat (gm)—5 or 8% daily value; saturated fat (gm)—0; sodium (mg)—358; cholesterol (mg)—0; carbohydrates (gm)—84; dietary fiber (gm)—12; protein (gm)—18. Analysis includes suggested side dishes.

Shiitake, Tofu, and Miso Sandwich with Pickled Ginger

Serves 4

1 teaspoon light olive oil with a dash of toasted sesame oil
12 fresh or softened dried shiitake mushrooms, stems removed
1/8 teaspoon white pepper
10 ounces light tofu, cut into 4 slices
1/8 teaspoon Shanghai Coastline Ethmix, divided (page 215)
4 (4-ounce or 114-gm) crusty rolls, cut horizontally almost through
4 teaspoons miso
4 teaspoons freshly squeezed lemon juice
12 thin slices pickled ginger

Heat the oil in a frying pan. Add the mushrooms, sprinkle with the white pepper, and press down on each with a spatula. Cook just to heat through, about 1 minute. Remove the mushrooms and lay the slices of tofu into the juices left in the pan. Dust lightly with 1/16 teaspoon of the homemade or purchased Shanghai Spice Mix and fry for 2 minutes. Turn and dust the other side with the remaining seasoning mix, cooking for another 2 minutes.

Pinch out about 1 ounce of bread from the center of each roll. Stir the miso and lemon juice together in a small bowl and spread both halves of each roll with 1 teaspoon of the mixture. Lay a slice of tofu on the bottom half of each roll. Place 3 mushrooms and 3 thin slices of ginger on top. Close the roll and grill for 5 minutes to heat through. Serve with the Mexican Cucumber (page 27) alongside.

Time Estimate: Preparation, 15 minutes; cooking, 5 minutes

Nutritional Profile per Serving: Calories—341; % calories from fat—15%; fat (gm)—6 or 9% daily value; saturated fat (gm)—1; sodium (mg)—779; cholesterol (mg)—0; carbohydrates (gm)—60; dietary fiber (gm)—5; protein (gm)—15. Analysis includes suggested side dishes.

White Bean and Green Chili Quesadillas

If you need to limit your salt intake, I suggest you use corn tortillas in this recipe. Corn tor-tillas have less than half the amount of salt of whole wheat tortillas and about a third that of flour tortillas. Look at page 40 to learn more about the compression grill.

Serves 4

1 (15-ounce or 425-gram) can Great Northern beans, drained and rinsed
1/2 teaspoon ground cumin
8 (8¼-inch or 20-cm) whole wheat tortillas
4 teaspoons chopped pickled jalapeños
1/2 cup diced green chilies
1/4 cup canned black beans, rinsed and drained
2 Roma tomatoes, thinly sliced
3/4 cup shredded nonfat sharp Cheddar cheese or 1/2 cup real Cheddar
16 cilantro leaves, roughly chopped
1/8 teaspoon salt

Garnish
1/4 cup yogurt cheese (page 210)

Preheat the grill on high for 10 minutes. Stir the cumin into the white beans. Lay 4 tortillas on a flat surface (reserving the remaining tortillas) and divide the white beans among them. Mash the beans with a fork and spread to within 1/2 inch (1.25 cm) of the edge of each tortilla. Sprinkle each with 1 teaspoon of the jalapeños and spread evenly over the beans. Now layer on each tortilla 2 tablespoons of the diced chilies and 1 tablespoon of the black beans. Lay tomato slices around the outside edge of the beans and sprinkle 3 tablespoons of the cheese and 1/4 of the cilantro over everything. Lighly dust with salt. Wet the rim of each layered tortilla and lay one of the reserved tortillas on top, pressing around the edge to seal. You can start to assemble the other three while you grill this one for 4 minutes. These can be baked ahead and reheated when you are ready to serve.

Note: If you don't have a compression grill, simply oven-broil or pan-broil for 3 minutes per side.

To serve: Cut the quesadillas into 8 wedges and lay them on a plate with a mound of Black Bean Salsa (page 26) in the center and a dollop of yogurt cheese on the side.

Time Estimate: Preparation, 20 minutes; unsupervised, 16 minutes

Nutritional Profile per Serving*

	White Bean Quesadilla	Classic Quesadilla	White Bean Quesadilla with Real Cheddar
Calories	414	1614	434
Fat (gm)	5	111	10
% Daily value of fat	8%	171%	16%
Saturated fat (gm)	less than 1	52	3
Calories from fat	11%	62%	19%
Cholesterol (mg)	4	238	15
Sodium (mg)	821	1996	774
Fiber (gm)	10	8	10
Carbohydrates (gm)	74	84	73
Protein (gm)	23	71	20

*Analysis includes suggested side dish.

The Cedar Plank

Wood plank and wood stick cooking were used by the earliest peoples of the Pacific Northwest. Not only does the wood season the food, giving it a subtle smoky flavor, but food cooked over wood prepares fast and stays juicy. Unfortunately, the wood plank usually lasted for only a few meals. That is, until a Pacific Northwest resident began a successful cottage industry with an aromatic cedar plank that's engineered to hang together.

All you have to do is oil it, never bake at more than 350°F (180°C), and tighten the stainless steel bolts when you see the cracks appear, as surely they will. The plank comes in two sizes. The first is an individual serving platter 9 × 13 × 1½ inches (23 cm × 33 cm × 4 cm) on which fish, meat, or fowl, roasted vegetables, and mushrooms can all be oven-baked and taken directly to the table. The larger size comes in either cedar or alder and is longer but narrower (7 × 17 × 1.5 inches or 18 cm × 43 cm × 4 cm); it makes a great presentation platter.

These planks are not inexpensive (at about $45 each) but they do the job and with very little special care should last for years. Unlike fine porcelain, they bounce if they are dropped!

graham discovers why the "super extra jumbo" Cedar plank never was very popular

One other element about the cedar plank really got my attention. In the instruction booklet I was encouraged to preheat the plank for 10 minutes at 350°F (180°C). I wondered why. To release the aromatic oils, perhaps? It turns out that since wood is porous, it can absorb meat juices like any chopping board. This could (if not properly cleansed) become unhygienic. Lo and behold—10 minutes at 350°F actually sterilizes the wood!

Any of the dishes that call for a cedar plank can be cooked in a glass or metal baking dish. Just add a few drops of chipotle sauce for the smoky flavor.

The Wooden Plank for Oven-Cooked Smoky Food

Can be alder or cedar

Carved "bowl" to retain juices. Occasionally sandpaper to revive the wood aromas.

Stainless steel bolts and nuts which can be tightened as you go; to compress the inevitable splits.

Cedar-Roasted Vegetable Sandwich

Serves 4

1/2 head garlic

1 large (4-ounce or 114-gm) portobello mushroom, sliced

1 medium zucchini squash, sliced on the diagonal

1/2 red onion, thinly sliced

2 Roma tomatoes, halved lengthwise, seeds squeezed out

2 Anaheim chilies, seeded and cored

1 delicata squash, peeled, seeded, and thinly sliced

1/4 teaspoon dried thyme

1/4 teaspoon salt

1/4 teaspoon freshly ground black pepper

4 long branches fresh rosemary

1 loaf (1 pound or 454 gm) crusty French or Italian bread

Sauce

1/4 cup yogurt cheese (page 210)

2 teaspoons Dijon mustard

1/2 teaspoon balsamic vinegar

Preheat the oven to 350°F (180°C). Place the cedar plank into the preheated oven to heat for 15 minutes. Cut off and discard the top third of the garlic head. Wrap the garlic in a small piece of aluminum foil and bake for 35 minutes while the plank is heating and the vegetables are cooking.

When the plank is hot, lay the mushroom slices, zucchini, onion, and tomatoes in the center well. Place the chilies and squash slices around the edges. Sprinkle the thyme, salt, and pepper over all the vegetables. Spread the rosemary branches on top. Bake in the preheated oven for 25 minutes.

To make the sauce: Combine the yogurt cheese, mustard, and balsamic vinegar in a small bowl. Remove the garlic from the foil, press down with a knife, and squeeze out all the soft roasted garlic. Add the garlic to the sauce and stir to mix.

Cut the loaf of bread lengthwise but not all the way through. Pull out some of the soft bread in the middle of both sides, leaving a well for the roasted vegetables. Spread both sides with the sauce. When the vegetables are tender, slice the chilies across diagonally, discarding the stem and large clump of seeds at the top. Fill the prepared loaf with the roasted vegetables, wrap loosely in foil and heat through in the hot oven for about 15 minutes. Slice into 8 thick slices and serve.

Time Estimate: Preparation, 20 minutes; unsupervised, 40 minutes

Nutritional Profile per Serving: Calories—418; % calories from fat—22%; fat (gm)—10 or 16% daily value; saturated fat (gm)—3; sodium (mg)—294; cholesterol (mg)—68; carbohydrates (gm)—54; dietary fiber (gm)—9; protein (gm)—30

Meat and Fish Entrees

Poêle or Étouffée (Shallow-Fry and Steam)

This is really a *method* of cooking, but it does need important design considerations when it comes to the cookware.

The method begins with a light sauté in very light oil. The shallow-fried meat or fish is surrounded by aromatic flavor enhancers like onions, garlic, ginger, or, in the case of the following recipe, by powerful Thai herbs. To this is added a small amount of stock: de-alcoholized wine, fruit juice, or other flavorful liquid. A heat-proof, dome-shaped lid is placed in the pan to create a part poaching/part steaming environment. The food cooks quickly with flavor and succulence. This is a truly swift method which encourages fat reduction and creativity.

Since this method uses one pan for four servings, and delicate foods such as fish fillets are often cooked this way, it means that the pan must be as large as possible.

Thai-Flavored Scallops with Shrimp and Artichoke Hearts

Serves 4

1½ pounds (680 gm) russet potatoes, peeled and cut into large chunks

1/2 pound (227 gm) sweet potato, peeled and cut into large chunks

Zest of 1/2 lemon, cut into strips

1 tablespoon chopped lemon grass

15 small fresh basil leaves

4 Kaffir lime leaves

1/2 teaspoon light olive oil with a dash of toasted sesame oil

4 small whole dried red chilies

2 cups fish stock (209)

4 tablespoons freshly squeezed lemon juice

1 pound (454 gm) bay scallops, laid on paper towels to dry

1/16 teaspoon white pepper

1 tablespoon arrowroot mixed with 2 tablespoons water (slurry)

1 (13¾-ounce or 385-gm) can artichoke hearts, drained and quartered

1/4 pound (114 gm) cooked and shelled baby shrimp

Garnish

1 tablespoon chopped fresh basil

1 ripe papaya, peeled, seeded, and cut into strips

4 butter lettuce leaves

Boil the white and sweet potatoes for 20 minutes. Drain off the water, place a clean dish towel in the pan on top of the potatoes, and allow to dry out on a warm burner. When the surfaces look mealy, press them through a ricer or sieve into a warm bowl. Mix well to even out the color. Keep warm.

Bruise the lemon zest, lemon grass, 5 of the basil leaves, and the lime leaves with the back of a knife. Place in a heated high-sided skillet with the oil and the chilies. Stir for 3 minutes over medium high heat to release the flavorful oils. Tip into a saucepan, pour in the fish stock, and bring to a boil. Allow it to reduce by one fourth. Strain 1 cup of the liquid into one container and the remaining 1/2 cup into another.

Reheat the high-sided skillet, without washing it, over medium high heat. Pour 2 tablespoons of the lemon juice into the pan and add the scallop slices in one layer. Cover and cook for 2 minutes. Drain the accumulated juices into the larger container of fish stock; add 2 more tablespoons of lemon juice to the scallops and let them brown slightly, uncovered, for 2 more minutes. Scatter the white pepper over the top.

Add the arrowroot slurry to the cup of fish stock and stir to mix. Tip the skillet, pushing the scallops aside, and pour the stock into one side of the pan. Return to the heat, stirring and shaking the pan until the sauce thickens, about 30 seconds. Add the remaining basil leaves, artichoke hearts, and shrimp, stirring gently to mix. If you think the sauce is too thick, thin it with 1/4 cup water.

To serve: Moisten the potatoes with the remaining 1/2 cup of stock and spoon into a pastry bag with a large star tip. Pipe the potatoes in the shape of a scallop shell on one side of each serving plate. Make a mound of scallops and shrimp opposite the potatoes or in scallop shells, if you have them. Place Steamed Bok Choy (page 151) on one side and papaya slices on a butter lettuce leaf on the other. Spoon the sauce onto the seafood and potatoes.

Time Estimate: Preparation, 25 minutes; cooking, 30 minutes

Nutritional Profile per Serving: Calories—366; % calories from fat—6%; fat (gm)—3 or 4% daily value; saturated fat (gm)—0; sodium (mg)—541; cholesterol (mg)—58; carbohydrates (gm)—72; dietary fiber (gm)—9; protein (gm)—18. Analysis includes suggested side dishes.

Once in a great while, I get a real shock when we do a nutritional analysis on a recipe. I thought canned artichoke hearts would be a delicious and harmless addition to this dish. I was very surprised to learn that they add 292 grams of sodium. If hypertension is a problem for you, I suggest you replace the artichoke hearts with hearts of bok choy. Here's how. After you steam the accompanying bok choy, cut the bottom 2 inches (5 cm) or so off each one. They will hold together somewhat like artichoke hearts and can be stirred in at the last minute in their place.

Tuna Kebabs

Serves 4

Sauce

1/2 teaspoon light olive oil with a dash of toasted sesame oil
1 clove garlic, peeled, bashed, and chopped
1 teaspoon freshly grated gingerroot
6 tablespoons de-alcoholized white wine, divided
2 tablespoons low-sodium tamari sauce
1 teaspoon brown sugar
1 teaspoon Shanghai Coastline Ethmix (page 215)
2 tablespoons unsalted creamy peanut butter, oil poured off

Kebabs

1 pound (454 gm) fresh tuna cut into 20 (1-inch or 2.5-cm) pieces
1 (8½-ounce or 240-gm) can whole artichoke hearts (8 hearts), drained and cut into halves

Garnish

3 tablespoons chopped cilantro or parsley

Set 4 bamboo skewers to soak in warm water. Preheat the compression grill (page 40) for 10 minutes.

For the sauce: Heat the oil in a small saucepan over medium high heat and fry the garlic and ginger for 2 minutes to release the flavorful oils. Add 1/4 cup of the wine, the tamari, brown sugar, and homemade or purchased Shanghai Spice Mix. Remove from the heat and add the peanut butter, stirring until smooth. Set aside and keep warm.

For the tuna kebabs: String 5 tuna pieces and 4 artichoke halves alternately on each bamboo skewer, starting and ending with tuna. Brush the kebabs with the sauce. Spray the grill with vegetable oil cooking spray and lay the kebabs on the grill. Close the lid and grill for 3 minutes. If you don't have a compression grill, simply oven-broil the kebabs for 3 minutes per side or until the tuna is white throughout.

Add the remaining wine to the rest of the sauce to thin it to a pouring consistency.

To serve: Divide Shanghai Spinach Rice (page 165) among 4 hot plates in a long narrow bed in the middle of each plate. Place a kebab on top of the rice. I like to serve Cantaloupe Salad strips (page 26) on either side. Pour sauce over the kebab and rice. Sprinkle chopped cilantro or parsley on top.

Time Estimate: Preparation, 15 minutes; cooking, 5 minutes

Nutritional Profile per Serving: Calories—526; % calories from fat—11%; fat (gm)—6 or 10% daily value; saturated fat (gm)—1; sodium (mg)—473; cholesterol (mg)—66; carbohydrates (gm)—72; dietary fiber (gm)—6; protein (gm)—44. Analysis includes suggested side dishes.

The Outdoor Electric Grill

The longer I'm involved with "variety from the lighter side," the more I've come to appreciate the value of lower-temperature, moisture-retaining cooking techniques. Whilst I enjoy the charbroiled crustiness of the BBQ, I prefer the tender succulence of the less aggressive method offered by the electric grill.

law of barbeque smoke direction:

figure 1

figure 2

cook stands to west of grill

cook moves to east of grill

Grilling on an electric grill concentrates flavor and moisture, making a virtual hassle-free environment that won't cause your neighbors, or yourself for that matter, the slightest distress. The surface heats to temperatures of over 400°F (200°C), which can deliver the characteristic grill bar markings and yet avoid the shriveling heat, fat flareups, and flavor-masking charred flesh. Grilled vegetables cooked in this manner are truly excellent and seafood is a real delight. It's well worth the investment, especially in condominiums or apartments that prohibit open fires on patios and balconies.

The "turtle" (which is what I call my electric grill because of its oval shell) is constructed for the most part of tough plastic and a very little rustproof metalwork. Mine is kept outside, with a special optional cover, on a patio that faces due west into the teeth of blustery winter gales that occasionally envelop our home in salt spray. It shows no signs of wear and tear. The oval ribbed grill surface is nonstick and completely removable to take to a large sink for an easy cleanup.

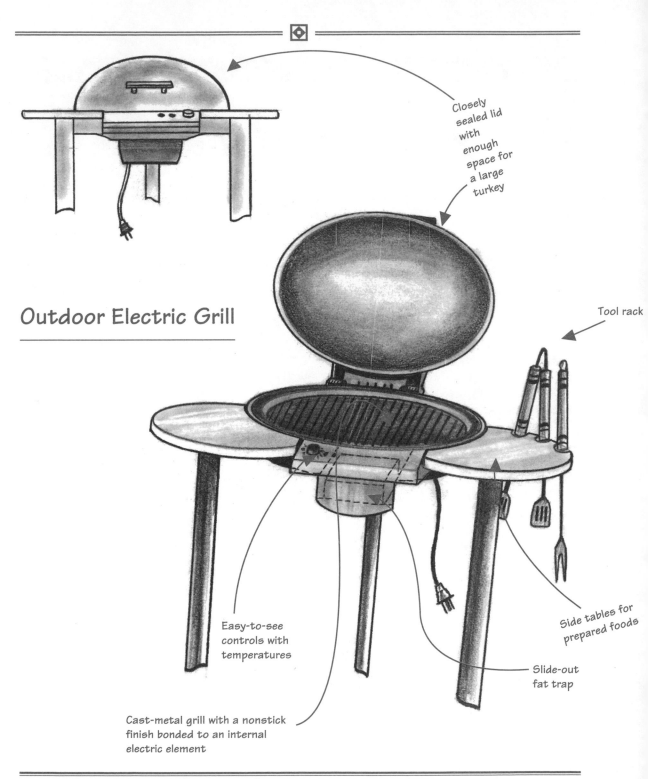

Outdoor Electric Grill

Closely sealed lid with enough space for a large turkey

Tool rack

Easy-to-see controls with temperatures

Side tables for prepared foods

Slide-out fat trap

Cast-metal grill with a nonstick finish bonded to an internal electric element

Grilled Trout

Serves 4

4 small whole trout (7 ounces or 200 gm each)
1/4 teaspoon salt, divided
1/4 teaspoon freshly ground white pepper, divided
1/8 teaspoon ground rosemary
1 lemon, thinly sliced (12 slices)
1½ teaspoons light olive oil with a dash of toasted sesame oil
1½ cups frozen corn kernels, thawed

1/2 cup de-alcoholized Chardonnay wine
2 tablespoons freshly squeezed lemon juice
1 tablespoon cornstarch mixed with 1/4 cup de-alcoholized Chardonnay wine (slurry)
1/4 cup yogurt cheese (page 210)
Garnish
2 tablespoons chopped fresh parsley

Preheat the grill over high heat for 15 minutes. If you choose to serve the trout with the suggested grilled vegetables, check the recipes for cooking times.

To bone the trout: Place the fish belly side down on a cutting board and gently but firmly press down on the spine to loosen the flesh from the backbone. Cut through the backbone at the head and tail, leaving both tail and head attached. Run a filet knife or other small, flexible blade along the spine toward the belly, close to the rib bones. Cut from the head to the tail end with the back of the blade next to the backbone and the blade close to the rib bones so that the flesh is cut away from the bones. Pull up on the backbone from the tail toward the head, lifting the bones from the flesh. Lay each fish open and lightly dust with 1/8 teaspoon of the salt and white pepper and the rosemary. Overlap 3 thin lemon slices down the center of each fish and close the fish, pinching the lemon slices in half. Put the oil on a plate and dust with salt and white pepper. Lay the trout on the plate and roll to coat the skin on both sides.

For the sauce: Whiz the corn and the wine in a blender until smooth. Pour into a bowl through a sieve and press to remove any pulp. Add the remaining salt and white pepper, the lemon juice, and the slurry, stirring to blend. Heat slowly over medium heat, stirring constantly while the sauce thickens. Pour the hot sauce slowly into the yogurt cheese, stirring with a whisk until smooth.

To cook the trout: Spray the grill with cooking spray and place the fish on the grill for 3 minutes on each side.

To serve: Place a trout on a hot plate with a grilled sweet potato half (page 166), one grilled zucchini half and one grilled summer squash half (page 159). Spoon sauce over the fish and sprinkle the parsley over the length of the trout.

Time Estimate: Preparation, 30 minutes; cooking, 6 minutes

Nutritional Profile per Serving: Calories—382; % calories from fat—24%; fat (gm)—10 or 16% daily value; saturated fat (gm)—3; sodium (mg)—286; cholesterol (mg)—98; carbohydrates (gm)—35; dietary fiber (gm)—5; protein (gm)—39. Analysis includes suggested side dishes.

The Microwave Oven

In 1974 I served as an adjunct professor at the Cornell University Hotel School. During this time my senior class undertook a practical survey of the microwave oven and its ability to produce cooked food that would match the textural qualities of food cooked by classic—albeit slower—culinary methods.

Of the two dozen or so techniques investigated, only one was equal to the classic "standard" qualities: poached fish and seafood (see recipes on the following pages). Clearly, microwave ovens have improved in the past twenty years. However, the basic cooking methodology has remained the same and it does alter the texture of many foods.

This academic study notwithstanding, I find the microwave to be a very useful piece of equipment because it heats my china teapot and dinner plates; it softens my homemade, low-sugar, nonfat frozen yogurt; it defrosts my forgotten dinner meats; and it begins the process of baking potatoes and winter squash.

I'm *sure* there are plenty of other excellent ideas in addition to those I've mentioned, but this isn't a book about microwaves alone, so I'll hasten on to detail some points to look for in a microwave.

some uses for your microwave

perfect hot tea

soften frozen yogurt

"start" baked potatoes

defrost frozen meat

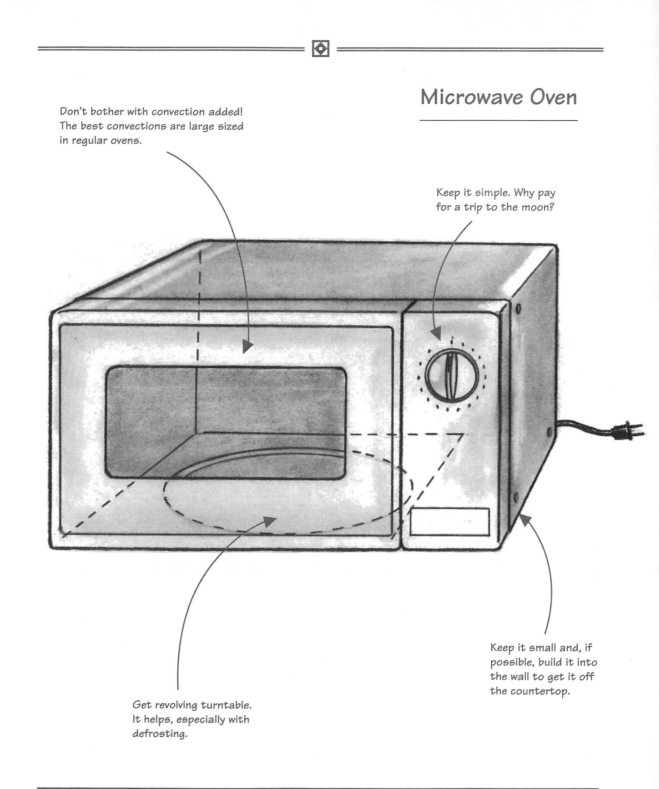

Don't bother with convection added!
The best convections are large sized
in regular ovens.

Keep it simple. Why pay
for a trip to the moon?

Get revolving turntable.
It helps, especially with
defrosting.

Keep it small and, if
possible, build it into
the wall to get it off
the countertop.

Sea Bass Fillets Bathed in Saffron Lemon Juice

Serves 4

1/4 cup freshly squeezed lemon juice
1/4 cup de-alcoholized Chardonnay wine
1/8 teaspoon salt
1/2 teaspoon dried dill
4 (6-ounce or 170-gm) sea bass fillets
1 teaspoon capers
Pinch of saffron
1 teaspoon arrowroot mixed with
    2 teaspoons de-alcoholized Chardonnay wine (slurry)

Garnish
Pinch of paprika
1/16 teaspoon white pepper

Combine the lemon juice, wine, salt, and dill in an 8 × 8-inch (20 × 20-cm) microwavable glass dish. Bathe the fish fillets in the liquid and cover the dish loosely with waxed paper. Microwave for 4 minutes on high power. When the fish is done, remove it from the microwave and pour the cooking liquid into a small saucepan, leaving the waxed paper over the fish to keep it warm. Add the capers to the cooking liquid and place over medium high heat until nice and hot. Stir a mere suspicion of saffron into the arrowroot slurry. Pull the sauce off the heat, pour in the slurry, then reheat until the sauce is thickened and clear.

To serve: Divide the fish fillets among 4 hot dinner plates. Spoon the sauce over the fish and sprinkle a little paprika and the white pepper on each one. Serve with Potato Halves with Parmesan Yogurt Sauce (page 162), Steamed Broccoli (page 151), and Steamed Acorn Squash slices (page 157).

Time Estimate: Preparation, 10 minutes; cooking, 5 minutes

Nutritional Profile per Serving: Calories—457; % calories from fat—10%; fat (gm)—5 or 8% daily value; saturated fat (gm)—1; sodium (mg)—471; cholesterol (mg)—145; carbohydrates (gm)—64; dietary fiber (gm)—10; protein (gm)—41. Analysis includes suggested side dishes.

Catfish

A little warmer please

Farmed channel catfish is firm textured, sweet flavored, white fleshed, and—get this—there are *no bones* in the fillets. A 6-ounce fillet has about 5 grams of fat, most of it mono-unsaturated.

In the early 1980s we consumed about 80 million pounds of catfish a year, largely in the southern states of America. This number has now gone through the roof, with close to 439 million pounds produced in 1996.

The fish of our nostalgic past came from quiet streams and muddy lake beds. Unfortunately, certain chemicals running off the land into our rivers have found their way into river catfish in excess of allowed safe amounts. This has encouraged the creation of an entire farming industry devoted to raising pollutant-free catfish.

I would like to tell you about a supplier from north of the Mason Dixon line. Just off the Snake River in Idaho, there is an outfit called Fish Breeders of Idaho, Inc., located in a small town called Buhl. They began in 1973 to tap the water of the geothermal springs at a stable 94°F and mix it with water from a cold spring to get an exact 83°F, the best growth/health range for catfish. The catfish thrive in this naturally oxygenated, chemical-free environment. This farm, along with fifteen Southern catfish farms, has earned the Catfish Institute's "Certified Processor" seal. Catfish with this seal are raised with stringent quality controls, ensuring that you will receive a premium product.

I'd love for you to give it a try by using this swift recipe. Catfish will keep well in your freezer and could become a fish favorite from the lighter end of the scale.

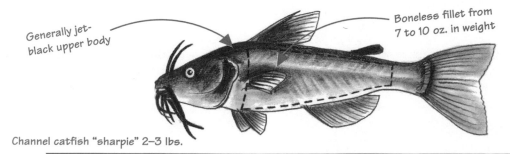

Generally jet-black upper body

Boneless fillet from 7 to 10 oz. in weight

Channel catfish "sharpie" 2–3 lbs.

Catfish with Creole Quinoa

Serves 4

2 delicata or small butternut squash, cut in half lengthwise, seeds removed

Creole quinoa
1 teaspoon light olive oil with a dash of toasted sesame oil
1 cup finely chopped onion
1/2 cup chopped celery
3 cloves garlic, peeled, bashed, and chopped
1 teaspoon dried thyme
1/8 teaspoon ground cloves
1/4 teaspoon ground red pepper (cayenne)
1/4 teaspoon salt, divided
2 bay leaves
1½ cups low-sodium chicken stock (page 207)
1 cup quinoa, well rinsed

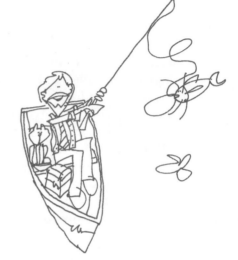

4 (6-ounce or 170-gm) catfish fillets
1/8 teaspoon ground white pepper

Sauce
1/4 cup mashed squash (from the 2 squash above)
1/2 cup de-alcoholized fruity white wine (such as Ariél Blanc)
1/8 teaspoon salt
1/8 teaspoon freshly ground black pepper
2 tablespoons yogurt cheese (page 210)

Garnish
1 tablespoon finely chopped fresh parsley

Preheat your oven to 450°F (230°C). Place the squash halves in a roasting pan in the middle of the preheated oven, skin side up, and cook for 25 minutes or until the flesh is soft. Remove 1 tablespoon of cooked squash from each half, mash and set aside for the sauce.

To prepare the quinoa: Heat the oil in a large, high-sided skillet over medium high heat and fry the onion until it begins to wilt, 2 minutes. Add the celery and garlic and cook 1 minute more. Sprinkle with the thyme, cloves, cayenne, 1/8 teaspoon of the salt, and the bay leaves. Pour in the stock and bring to a boil. Add the quinoa, cover, and simmer for 10 minutes.

Fill the baked squash halves with the quinoa and lay a catfish fillet on top of each, tucking in the ends so they don't hang over the edge. Set on a broiler pan, spray very lightly with olive oil cooking spray, and sprinkle with 1/8 teaspoon of the salt and the white pepper. Broil for 8 minutes.

To make the sauce: Combine the mashed squash with the wine and a pinch of salt and pepper in a 2-cup glass measure and heat over hot water. Off the heat, stir in the yogurt cheese until the sauce is smooth.

To serve: Place a fish-topped squash half on each of 4 hot plates and serve with Steamed Spinach (page 157) and Broiled Tomatoes (page 161). Spoon a little of the sauce over the spinach and scatter parsley over the top.

Time Estimate: Preparation, 20 minutes; cooking, 26 minutes; unsupervised, 15–20 minutes, depending on oven

Nutritional Profile per Serving: Calories—496; % calories from fat—18%; fat (gm)—10 or 15% daily value; saturated fat (gm)—2; sodium (mg)—479; cholesterol (mg)—99; carbohydrates (gm)—66; dietary fiber (gm)—13; protein (gm)—42. Analysis includes suggested side dishes.

Each grain of quinoa, pronounced KEEN-wah, is covered with a resinlike substance called saponin, which serves as a natural protection from rodents and insects. Most of this bitter coating has been removed before it reaches the store but this grain should be rinsed before you cook it. Place the quinoa in a strainer and run cold water over it until the water runs clear.

The Convection Oven

In a convection oven, the heat increases with fan-driven air. The wind factor drives up the temperature by about 50°F at a 300° to 400° range so you can reduce your normal temperature of about 350° (180°C) for roast chicken to 300°F. You will also find that cooking times will be reduced by about 30 percent and there is no need to preheat the oven—all of which are time and energy saving.

Because the air is extracted through the heating elements, atomized fatty particles are incinerated. Those that do attach are converted by special side panels into water and carbon dioxide, which is immediately extracted.

It's an integrated, well-thought-out system that qualifies for *swift* not only because it saves some time but because it also gets wonderful results.

The recipe that follows uses convection coupled with a glazed clay pylon. Because the hot air is blown about so evenly it means that the chicken virtually spit-roasts and *internally* bakes, resulting in incredible moisture and enhanced herb flavor.

Must you have a new oven and the clay pylon? No. We are discussing greater ease and superb results. You can take a little longer, using your regular oven, and possibly more easily locate a wire vertical roaster. It should still give you the best roast chicken you've had in years.

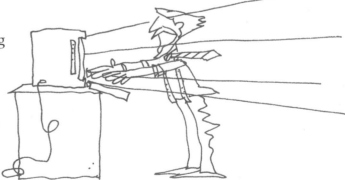

graham tests the wind factor in his new convection oven

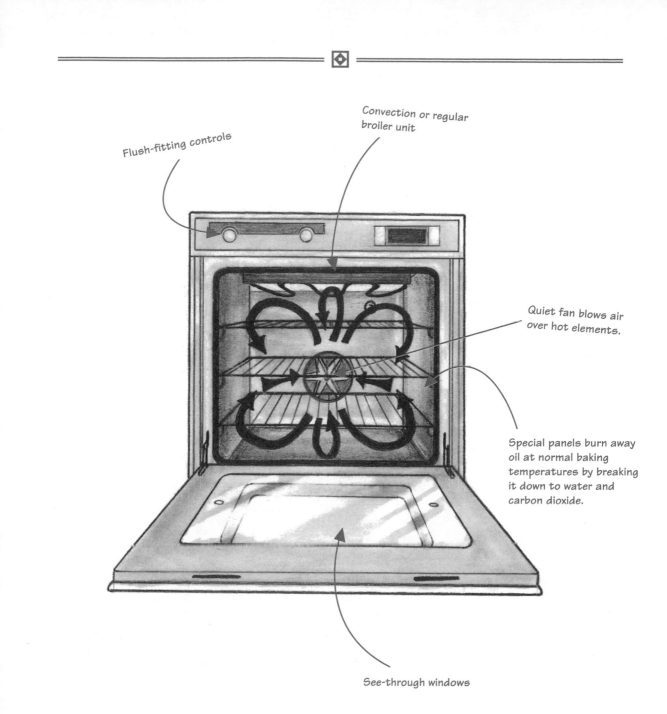

Flush-fitting controls

Convection or regular broiler unit

Quiet fan blows air over hot elements.

Special panels burn away oil at normal baking temperatures by breaking it down to water and carbon dioxide.

See-through windows

The Convection Oven

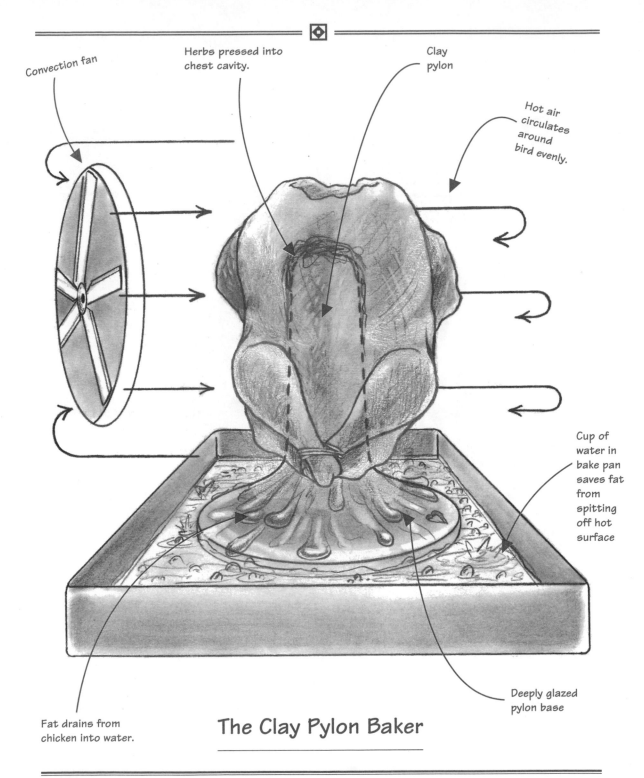

Convection fan

Herbs pressed into chest cavity.

Clay pylon

Hot air circulates around bird evenly.

Cup of water in bake pan saves fat from spitting off hot surface

Deeply glazed pylon base

Fat drains from chicken into water.

The Clay Pylon Baker

Roasted Chicken

Serves 4

1 (3½-pound or 1.6-kg) broiler/fryer chicken
2 tablespoons freshly squeezed lemon juice
1/8 teaspoon salt
1/8 teaspoon freshly ground black pepper
2 (3-inch or 7-cm) sprigs fresh thyme
2 (3-inch or 7-cm) sprigs fresh rosemary
3 fresh sage leaves

Sauce
1/4 cup de-alcoholized red wine
2 teaspoons arrowroot mixed with
    4 teaspoons de-alcoholized red wine (slurry)

Preheat the convection oven to 350°F (180°C) or a conventional oven to 400°F (204°C).

To prepare the chicken: Remove the fat from around the body cavity and neck; remove and discard the first 2 joints of each wing. Rinse the chicken inside and out and pat dry with paper towels. Pour the lemon juice inside the body cavity and sprinkle the inside with salt and pepper. Lay the thyme, rosemary, and sage leaves inside. If you are using a clay pylon, insert the ceramic core to hold the herbs in place. Turn the pylon onto its base on a plate to catch the lemon juice. Cross the legs loosely over each other and tie together with cotton string. Brush the accumulated lemon juice over the outside of the chicken and place the bird in a 9 x 13-inch (23 x 33-cm) baking pan. Pour 1½ cups of water into the pan. Roast in the preheated convection oven for 40 minutes or until the chicken juices run clear. In a conventional oven, the chicken should be done in about an hour. Remove the chicken to a hot platter and allow to set for at least 10 minutes before carving.

> When you are working with raw poultry, please be very careful to use a separate cutting board. Wash your hands, your knives, and other utensils in hot soapy water. I know this sounds fussy, but you know how concerned I am about your good health. A bout with salmonella is no fun and can be easily avoided.

Take the chicken off the ceramic core, remove the skin, and carve into serving size pieces.

For the sauce: Pour the liquid into the roasting pan and deglaze it with the wine. Pour into a fat strainer and then pour the defatted liquid into a small saucepan. Stir in the slurry and stir over medium high heat until thickened.

To serve: Place a piece of chicken on each plate and pour some sauce over the top. Add a serving of Steamed Broccoli (page 151), Carrots in Tonic Water (page 152), and a Baked Russet Potato half (page 166).

Time Estimate: Preparation, 15 minutes; cooking, 3 minutes; unsupervised, 45 minutes

Nutritional Profile per Serving: Calories—451; % calories from fat—25%; fat (gm)—12 or 19% daily value; saturated fat (gm)—3; sodium (mg)—380; cholesterol (mg)—127; carbohydrates (gm)—39; dietary fiber (gm)—6; protein (gm)—47. Analysis includes suggested side dishes.

Shanghai Chicken Breast MEV

Please look at the description of MEVs on page 117 before you attempt this recipe. An MEV is usually meatless, thus its name Molded Ethnic Vegetables. I fill a flat–topped mold with layers of fillings which, when turned out on a plate, give the entree height and the plate a focus. In this recipe I've taken liberties with the vegetarian part of it and added chicken as one of the ingredients. I think you'll like it.

Serves 4

Marinade

1 cup de-alcoholized fruity white wine (I prefer Ariél Blanc)

3 tablespoons low-sodium tamari

1 tablespoon chopped garlic

1 teaspoon grated fresh gingerroot

3/4 teaspoon Shanghai Coastline Ethmix (page 215), divided

Filling

2 (6-ounce or 170-gm) boneless chicken breast halves, skin on

1 teaspoon light olive oil with a dash of toasted sesame oil

8 shiitake mushrooms, stemmed and chopped

16 canned water chestnuts, quartered

4 small sweet red peppers cut in 1-inch (2.5-cm) dice (you may substitute 1 red bell pepper)

1¼ cups Steamed Pearl Rice (page 163)

1 teaspoon arrowroot mixed with 1 tablespoon wine (slurry)

Combine the marinade ingredients and 1/2 teaspoon of the spice mix in a small saucepan. Bring to a boil and cook for 1 minute. Lay the chicken breasts on a plate, skin side down. Draw the marinade into a marinating syringe and inject as much of the marinade as you can into each breast, starting at the thick end. If you don't have a syringe, marinate the chicken for 30 minutes in the refrigerator.

Preheat the oven to 350°F (180°C). Heat the oil in a large high–sided skillet over medium high heat. Cook the chicken breasts, skin side down, for 2 minutes; reduce the heat to low and turn, pushing the chicken to one side of the pan. Add the chopped mushrooms, water chestnuts, diced peppers, and remaining seasoning mix. Stir and cook the vegetables for 2 minutes. Turn the chicken again and cook everything 2 more minutes. Place the chicken on a cutting board to remove and discard the skin. (The meat will finish cooking when you heat the MEV.) Tip the vegetables into a bowl and pour any remaining marinade—including the marinade left on the plate—into the pan. Scrape up the flavorful bits on the bottom of the pan and make sure the liquid comes to a full boil. Set aside.

Cut each of the chicken breasts into 4 large diagonal pieces. Spray 4 MEV or other 1-cup molds with vegetable oil cooking spray. Spoon 2 tablespoons of the cooked rice into each mold and press down. Lay 2 of the chicken chunks on the rice and divide the vegetables among the 4 molds. Set the last piece of chicken on the vegetables, spoon 2 tablespoons of marinade over each, and cap with 2 more tablespoons of rice. Heat for 15 to 20 minutes in the preheated oven. Add 1/2 cup water and the slurry to the marinade in the pan and heat until clear and thickened.

To serve: Place an MEV on each of 4 hot plates. I like to eat this one with whole Lemon Fried Shiitake mushrooms (page 156) and frozen baby lima beans cooked according to package directions. Pour the sauce around the MEV and a little extra on the lima beans.

Time Estimate: Preparation, 25 minutes; cooking, 8 minutes; unsupervised, 20 minutes

Nutritional Profile per Serving: Calories—444; % calories from fat—16%; fat (gm)—8 or 12% daily value; saturated fat (gm)—2; sodium (mg)—660; cholesterol (mg)—71; carbohydrates (gm)—55; dietary fiber (gm)—10; protein (gm)—37. Analysis includes suggested side dishes.

Stack and Steam

Steaming is swift with only minor leaching of water-soluble nutrients. Because of the speed of steam cooking, food colors are preserved, and when combined with either stacking or segmenting it makes the very best use of energy in its one-pot configuration.

The best steamers are stainless steel and come in two basic styles:

• Stacking: where two or three units sit on top of each other using one source of boiling water.

• Segmenting: where only one tray is used and is divided by two 90°-angled pieces of stainless steel.

The two styles can be united, giving more flexibility to the stacking versions (see accompanying illustration).

I like to use the steamer for fresh fish. I place the fillets (no larger than 6 ounces each) on a plate with appropriate seasonings and steam them for 6 to 8 minutes. The trick is to provide easy access to the plate, especially when it's hot and running with precious juices. This is where the design really matters.

• There must be enough room for an 8-inch plate, making a 10-inch diameter optimal.

• The steamer tray base must either be removable or

• Reversible

The smaller-sized self-contained electric steamers don't meet these criteria.

Stack (or Segment) and Steam

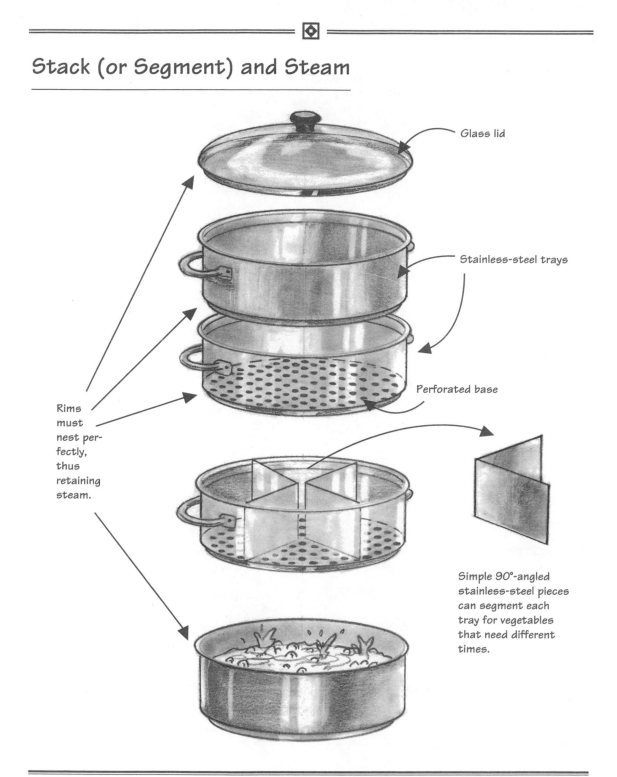

Glass lid

Stainless-steel trays

Perforated base

Rims must nest perfectly, thus retaining steam.

Simple 90°-angled stainless-steel pieces can segment each tray for vegetables that need different times.

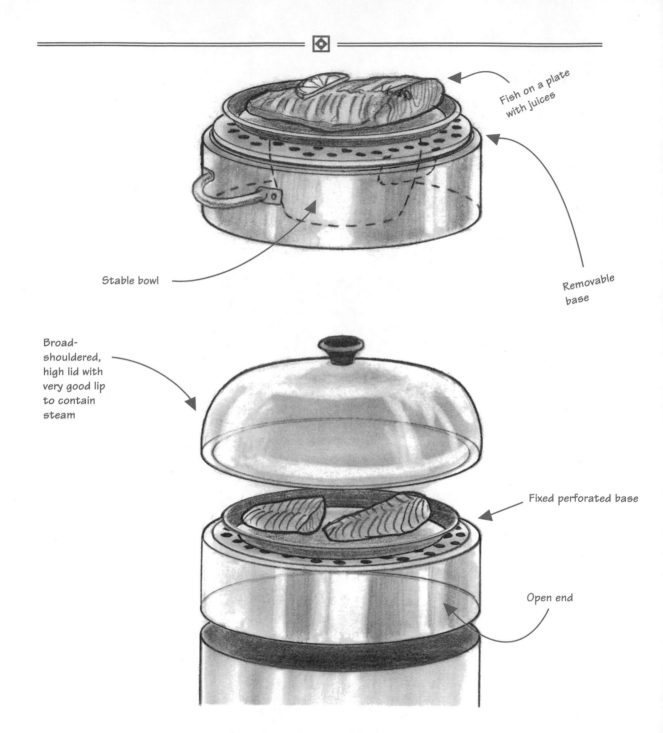

Fish on a plate with juices

Stable bowl

Removable base

Broad-shouldered, high lid with very good lip to contain steam

Fixed perforated base

Open end

This illustration shows a steamer tray that can be reversed.
The plate can be set on the base, where it can be picked up easily.

Steamed Chicken Strips with Carrots

Serves 4

12 ounces (340 gm) boneless skinless chicken breasts
2 tablespoons de-alcoholized Chardonnay wine
1/4 teaspoon Shanghai Coastline Ethmix (page 215)
1/8 teaspoon salt
3 large carrots, peeled
1/16 teaspoon white pepper

Sauce
1/2 cup low-sodium chicken stock
1/2 cup de-alcoholized Chardonnay
1 teaspoon dried tarragon
2 teaspoons arrowroot mixed with 1 tablespoon de-alcoholized Chardonnay (slurry)

Cut chicken into strips 3 inches long and 1/4-inch thick (7.5 cm × .6 cm) and spread them on a plate that will fit into your steamer. Combine the 2 tablespoons of wine, the spice mix, and the salt. Pour over the chicken and stir to mix thoroughly. Place the plate on a steaming platform and set aside.

Cut the carrots into strips the same size as the chicken. Place in a second steaming platform and sprinkle with the white pepper.

Bring 2 cups of water to a boil in your steamer. Place the platform with the carrots on the steamer, cover, and cook for 2 minutes over medium high heat. Put the carrot platform on top of the chicken platform and set both on the steamer. Steam, covered, for 4 minutes. When they are done, tip the chicken from the plate into the carrots and toss to mix.

To make the sauce: Pour the stock, wine, and tarragon into a small saucepan. Bring to a boil, remove from the heat, and stir in the arrowroot slurry. Return to the heat to clear and thicken (which will happen almost immediately).

To serve: Divide the chicken and carrots among 4 hot plates. Spoon the sauce over the chicken and it's ready! I like to serve this with Steamed Kale (page 155) and Couscous with Mint (page 158).

Time Estimate: Preparation, 15 minutes; cooking, 10 minutes

Nutritional Profile per Serving: Calories—318; % calories from fat—8%; fat (gm)—3 or 5% daily value; saturated fat (gm)—1; sodium (mg)—242; cholesterol (mg)—47; carbohydrates (gm)—46; dietary fiber (gm)—6; protein (gm)—28. Analysis includes suggested side dishes.

The Blender

Apparently, 94 percent of U.S. households own a blender, and they are often out there on valuable counter space doing their thing. If, by chance, you are one of the 6 percent who doesn't have a blender, then let me explain why I believe they belong in a *swift* kitchen.

A modern blender really can crush ice, make bread crumbs, reconstitute juice in a flash, "cream" soups, purée vegetables and fruits smooth enough for babies, make dips and batters, . . . and on and on.

The blender works especially well for making smooth vegetable sauces. I begin with 1 pound of a raw, unpeeled vegetable like parsnip, carrot, sweet potato, winter squash or peas, new lima beans—really, anything is possible! I then peel, cut roughly, and steam (page 76) it until quite tender, *almost* overcooked. I combine approximately 1½ cups of the cooked vegetable with a 12-ounce (354-ml) can of evaporated skim milk in the blender and fix the lid. Start at the lowest speed and build to purée.

A good blender will whip through this in only 2 to 3 minutes. Now add 1/2 cup of yogurt cheese if you want added dairy-style creaminess, and adjust the seasoning to your taste.

Some vegetables have stubborn skins or fibers and may need to be sieved before serving. I designed a tool for this purpose that works with a good stainless-steel hand sieve. I call it a sock 'n sieve because I think it looks like the old sock-darning implement that people used to mend socks rather than throw them out. You could use a wooden spoon or any nonmetal instrument to do the job. Just be careful not to the tear the sieve.

The Modern Blender

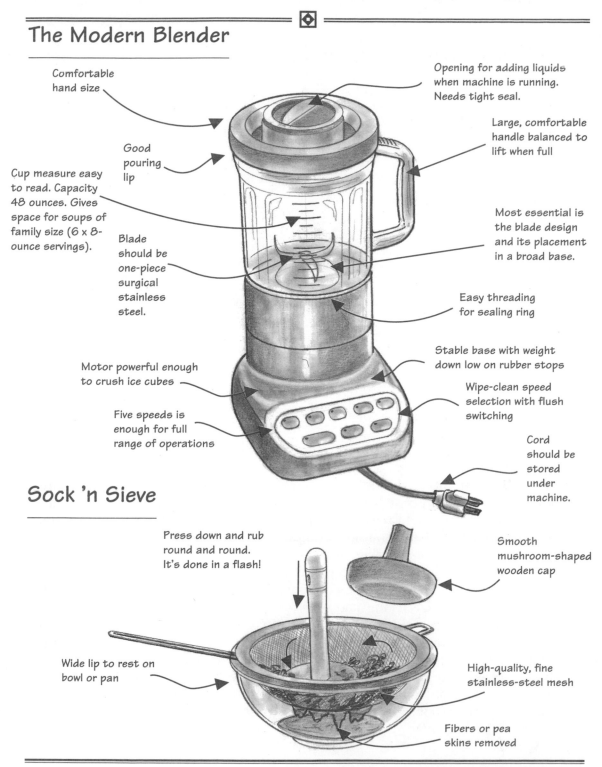

Comfortable hand size

Opening for adding liquids when machine is running. Needs tight seal.

Good pouring lip

Large, comfortable handle balanced to lift when full

Cup measure easy to read. Capacity 48 ounces. Gives space for soups of family size (6 x 8-ounce servings).

Blade should be one-piece surgical stainless steel.

Most essential is the blade design and its placement in a broad base.

Easy threading for sealing ring

Motor powerful enough to crush ice cubes

Stable base with weight down low on rubber stops

Wipe-clean speed selection with flush switching

Five speeds is enough for full range of operations

Cord should be stored under machine.

Sock 'n Sieve

Press down and rub round and round. It's done in a flash!

Smooth mushroom-shaped wooden cap

Wide lip to rest on bowl or pan

High-quality, fine stainless-steel mesh

Fibers or pea skins removed

Chicken Noodle Casserole

Serves 4

1/2 teaspoon light olive oil with a dash of toasted sesame oil
2 cloves garlic, peeled, bashed, and chopped
1 (15-ounce or 425-gm) can Great Northern beans, drained and rinsed
1 teaspoon Scandinavia Ethmix (page 215)
1/2 cup chicken stock
1 cup evaporated skim milk
2 tablespoons freshly squeezed lemon juice
12 mushrooms, sliced in thirds from top to bottom
1/8 teaspoon salt
1/8 teaspoon white pepper
10 ounces (280 gm) cooked chicken breast meat (prepared fresh, canned, or leftover)
2 cups frozen peas
1/4 cup chopped pimientos
2 tablespoons arrowroot mixed with 1/4 cup de-alcoholized Chardonnay (slurry)
8 ounces (227 gm) fast-cooking dry spinach fettuccine

Garnish
4 teaspoons freshly grated Parmesan cheese

Heat the oil in a high-sided frying pan over medium high heat. Add the garlic and cook just to release the flavorful oils, 1 minute. Add 1 cup of the beans and the spice mix and cook for 2 minutes to heat through. Place in a blender jar with the chicken stock and whiz for 1 full minute or until perfectly smooth. Pour the evaporated skim milk into the blender with the motor running on a slow speed. Set the sauce aside.

Pour the lemon juice over the sliced mushrooms and toss to mix. Heat a medium-size frying pan over medium high heat and add the mushrooms, which will brown nicely because of the lemon juice in about 3 or 4 minutes. Add the salt and pepper while the mushrooms are frying. Add the chicken, remaining beans, peas, and pimientos, then pour in the blended, smooth sauce. As soon as the sauce is hot, pull the pan off the heat, add the arrowroot slurry, and heat to provide a lovely gloss. Cover and keep warm.

Bring water to a boil in a large pot, add the pasta, and cook for 4 minutes. Drain through a colander, stir into the hot sauce, and dust with the Parmesan cheese.

Time Estimate: Preparation, 15 minutes; cooking, 10 minutes

Nutritional Profile per Serving: Calories—475; % calories from fat—9%; fat (gm)—5 or 11% daily value; saturated fat (gm)—1; sodium (mg)—419; cholesterol (mg)—69; carbohydrates (gm)—73; dietary fiber (gm)—9; protein (gm)—36. Analysis includes suggested side dishes.

Ostrich

This kind of popularity I can live without.

Be as popular as a turkey at thanksgiving!

The very earliest you will read these words could be January 1, 1997, about one year's delay since I wrote them. During that one year an estimated 20,000 laying ostrich hens will have laid an average of 40 eggs each. Of these 40, about 20 will hatch and survive to create 400,000 additional big birds.

Many of these will become breeding pairs and fetch somewhere between $15,000 and $20,000 as a reproductive couple. The rest will, after only 12 to 14 months, reach as high as 75 pounds of meat and 14 square feet of skin used for leather. By waiting an additional 48 months, the combined meat yield of the offspring of a breeding pair can be 1,750 pounds and 322 square feet of leather. Compare that to a 550-pound cow with 30 square feet of leather that takes 21 months from impregnation to market. The ever-increasing and swift production gives rise to the hope that the ostrich could soon become another turkey—popular, low-fat, *and* inexpensive.

According to James Muth in the *National Culinary Review* (March 1994), the good old turkey started out its career with a breeding price of over $2,000 in the 1920s. So we should see this as a truly encouraging sign for the future prices of ostrich. We are presented with an ever-decreasing cost per pound: It started as high as $30 for the most tender cuts, fell to $19 within two years, and today's price . . . well, why not call 1–800–652–0223 and check it out?

Hello? 1·800·652·0223?

Ostrich meat is cherry to dark red and is akin to beef in flavor and texture. It is, for the most part, extremely tender and flavorsome. Its sinew/gelatinous tendons dissolve in moist heat to produce magnificent stock. The long neck and its bones make truly world-class soups and neck stews, and the early tests on a summer sausage are excellent.

Now for the exceptional news: Its fat content is very low and yet, when compared side by side with well-marbled, choice cuts of beef, it still passes the critical taste test. Why not give it a go, just once, and see for yourself?

Nutritional Comparison of Meat
based on 3-oz. cooked portions

	Ostrich	Beef Tenderloin	Chicken Breast	Pacific Salmon	Venison	Bison
Calories	108	179	140	153	134	122
Fat (gm)	2	9	3	9	3	2
Cholest. (mg)	66	71	72	56	95	70
Protein (gm)	22	24	26	17	26	24

We are, of course, breaking new ground with ostrich, especially when trying to categorize various cuts as tender or tough or suited to roasting, grilling, or stewing. Some experimenting chefs have differing views which owe much to the methods of cooking used.

The Texas A&M Meat Science Department ran tenderness tests on different cuts of ostrich. The mechanical measurement of tenderness is called shear force. Less than 8 is regarded as very tender. Eight through 10 is acceptable, and 10 and over is tough. The only piece that edged into the tough range when cooked was outside leg (drum).

I've divided the ostrich into three very simple groups and given you a recipe for each.

• *Neck*—This makes a truly triumphant soup, easily the equal of the famed oxtail. It has wonderful collagen that melts into the soup, giving richness without fattiness. It is seldom marketed as such, often being trimmed for ground meat or discarded.

• *Drum*—This cut, also called the outside leg, has a shear force of 6 to 7. The toughest part is called the tip of the thigh and is used mostly for ground meat because of its firm 8.2 rating.

• *Thigh*—Because of its size and complexity, the thigh is usually divided into four tender cuts suitable for roasting, frying, grilling, or even sushi.

Cut	Shear Force
Inside strip	4.6
Top loin	5.9
Outside thigh	6.2
Fan	6.4

• *Back*—This part is often called the tenderloin. It is long and fairly flat and can be very tough at the larger end extremity. The smaller end of the tenderloin has a shear force of 5.4.

The time is ripe for some truly creative ideas that celebrate this healthy contender for the culinary crown.

Roast Ostrich with Tart Cherry Cabernet Sauce

Serves 6

1¼ pounds (567 gm) ostrich tenderloin, fan, or inside strip muscle
1/8 teaspoon salt
1/4 teaspoon freshly ground black pepper
1 shallot, peeled and cut into thin strips

Sauce
1 teaspoon light olive oil with a dash of toasted sesame oil
2 tablespoons chopped shallots (1 shallot)
1/4 cup dried tart cherries
1 cup de-alcoholized Cabernet Sauvignon
2 teaspoons arrowroot mixed with 4 teaspoons de-alcoholized Cabernet Sauvignon (slurry)
2 teaspoons chopped fresh parsley
1/8 teaspoon salt
1/8 teaspoon freshly ground black pepper

Garnish
2 tablespoons chopped fresh parsley

Preheat the oven to 350°F (180°C). Trim any tough white tissue from the tenderloin, dust it lightly with salt and pepper, and strew the shallots over the top. Lay the roast on a rack in a roasting pan and spray very lightly with olive oil cooking spray. Roast in the preheated oven for 25 minutes for medium rare. There is very little fat in ostrich meat, so it's important not to overcook it—red to pink is best!

While the roast is cooking, make the sauce. Heat the oil in a small saucepan over medium heat. Drop the chopped shallots into the pan and fry until they soften. Add the tart cherries and wine and simmer for 6 minutes. Tip the sauce into a blender and whiz until smooth. Press through a sieve into a small saucepan to remove the cherry skins and shallot pieces. Stir in the slurry and reheat in the small saucepan to clear and thicken. Add the parsley, salt, and pepper.

To serve: Slice the meat thinly and divide it among 6 hot plates. Spoon the dark red sauce over the meat; garnish with the chopped parsley.

Time Estimate: Preparation, 15 minutes; cooking, 7 minutes; unsupervised, 25 minutes

Nutritional Profile per Serving*

	Ostrich Tenderloin	Classic Beef Tenderloin
Calories	153	227
Fat (gm)	3	10
% Daily value of fat	5%	15%
Saturated fat (gm)	less than 1	4
Calories from fat	17%	40%
Cholesterol (mg)	73	79
Sodium (mg)	50	108
Fiber (gm)	less than 1	0
Carbohydrates (gm)	7	7
Protein (gm)	25	27

*While both numbers are reasonable, I do want you to compare these two red meats in order to see how low you can go. A serving of red meat at 5 percent of the daily value for fat seems like a miracle (if it weren't for the current price!).

Ostrich Osso Buco

Serves 4

1 teaspoon light olive oil with a dash of toasted sesame oil
2 pounds (908 gm) ostrich shank, cut 1 inch (2.5 cm) thick,
    yielding 1 pound trimmed meat
1½ cups diced onions (1/2-inch or 1.25-cm dice)
3 cloves garlic, peeled, bashed, and chopped
1 cup diced carrots (1/2-inch or 1.25-cm dice)
1 cup diced celery (1/2-inch or 1.25-cm dice)
1/2 cup low-sodium tomato purée
1/4 teaspoon salt
1/4 teaspoon freshly ground black pepper
1/2 cup de-alcoholized Chardonnay wine
1/2 cup no-salt beef broth or ostrich broth (page 208)
4 thyme sprigs
2 bay leaves
6 parsley stalks
2 tablespoons lemon juice
2 cups sliced mushrooms
1/2 teaspoon lemon zest
1 tablespoon arrowroot mixed with 2 tablespoons water (slurry)

Heat the oil in a pressure cooker or a high-sided skillet over high heat. Cut the sinew on the outside of each ostrich shank to prevent it from curling when cooked. Brown the pieces of meat, remove from the pan, and set aside. Put the onions in the pan and fry, stirring, until they are lightly colored, 30 seconds. Add the garlic, carrots, and celery and toss in the hot pan. Pour in the tomato purée, the salt, and pepper, and stir to mix. Nestle the meat into the vegetables and pour in the wine and broth. Tie the thyme sprigs, bay leaves, and parsley stalks in a square of cheesecloth to make a bouquet garni. Drop it into the pan, cover, and bring the pressure up to high. Turn the heat down and cook for 30 minutes, then quick-release. If you use a high-sided skillet, it will need to simmer, covered, for 3 hours to tenderize the meat.

Heat a large sauté pan over medium high heat. Pour in the lemon juice and add the mushrooms to brown for 1 or 2 minutes. Tip them into the osso buco with the lemon zest and stir to mix. Pour in the slurry and place on the heat to thicken and clear. Remove the bouquet garni before serving.

To serve: Divide among 4 hot bowls and add a scoop of rice or low-fat risotto.

Time Estimate: Preparation, 20 minutes; cooking, 7 minutes; unsupervised, 35 minutes in a pressure cooker or 3 hours in a conventional pan

Nutritional Profile per Serving*

	Ostrich Osso Buco	Classic Osso Buco
Calories	283	867
Fat (gm)	5	39
% Daily value of fat	8%	60%
Saturated fat (gm)	less than 1	11
Calories from fat	17%	41%
Cholesterol (mg)	87	383
Sodium (mg)	253	2299
Fiber (gm)	6	3
Carbohydrates (gm)	28	22
Protein (gm)	35	97

*This just happens to be one of my favorite former-life dishes in its classic form. I was really excited by the way in which ostrich mimics the rich smoothness of the veal shank, if not its pale color. The comparison clearly shows the wisdom of selecting lower-fat meats.

Pasta Is Swift

Swift is a mix of ease and speed, with ease having the priority. Part of swift is to be successful and to select foods and methods that preserve or present the highest possible nutritional values whilst retaining the pleasures of the eating experience.

Pasta is swift. When it's freshly made, it cooks in 2 to 4 minutes. When it's dried, it usually takes from 9 to 12 minutes, depending upon the size. Recently some very thinly sheeted, high-gluten, pastas have been sold in dried form which cook in 2 to 3 minutes like their "fresh" relatives.

To all this talk of speed, add the element of "highest possible nutritional value" and you stumble over a relatively new element—*enrichment*. By this I do not mean added micronutrients but the addition of a purée of peas that lifts the protein value of the pasta and provides both soluble and insoluble fiber. It is being made by a giant Italian manufacturer, Rummo, who has been making pasta since 1860 and has won awards for its quality.

To my taste, it's excellent. Whilst it loses the speed wars by a minute or two, it does increase complete protein without adding any animal fats and therefore it becomes *swift*.

The following chart provides some comparative numbers for you:

	Calories	Fat gm	Protein gm	Fiber gm	Sodium gm	Carbohydrates gm
Eggless Pasta (1 cup cooked)	189	1	6	2	1	38
Rummo Pasta (1 cup cooked)	190	<1	10	3	30	38
Potatoes (1 cup cooked)	136	0	3	3	6	31
Rice (1 cup cooked)	267	1	6	1	2	58
Halibut (4 oz. cooked)	149	3	25	0	78	0
Chicken Breast (4 oz. cooked)	223	9	34	0	81	0

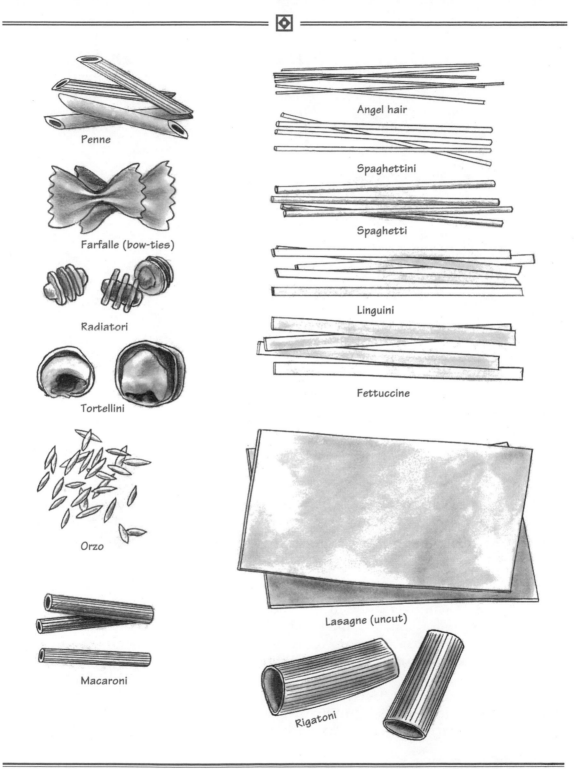

Penne

Farfalle (bow-ties)

Radiatori

Tortellini

Orzo

Macaroni

Angel hair

Spaghettini

Spaghetti

Linguini

Fettuccine

Lasagne (uncut)

Rigatoni

Penne with Italian Sausage and Sugar Peas

For the true aficionado, Viva Italia tomatoes are beautiful Italian sauce tomatoes. Unfortunately, they are not grown commercially, so you will have to grow your own. Check a seed catalogue or your local nursery.

Serves 4 generously

1 pound (452 gm) carrots, peeled, sliced, and cooked until soft
1 can (12 fluid ounces or 354 ml) evaporated skim milk
1 cup no-sodium chicken stock (page 207)
1/4 teaspoon white pepper
1/8 teaspoon salt
1 teaspoon Northwest Italy Ethmix (page 216)
12 ounces (340 gm) dry penne pasta
2 tablespoons freshly squeezed lemon juice
7 ounces (198 gm) low-fat turkey Italian sausage links, cut into 2 x 1/4-inch (5 x .64-cm) strips
1 bunch (about 6) green onions, trimmed and cut into 2-inch (5-cm) lengths, green and white parts separated
8 ounces (226 gm) sugar snap or Chinese snow pea pods, stems and strings removed
1 cup de-alcoholized Chardonnay wine

Garnish
4 tablespoons freshly grated Parmesan cheese
1 Roma or Viva Italia tomato, cut into thin (2 x 1/4-inch or 5 x .64-cm) strips

For the sauce: Put the carrots in a blender with 1/2 can evaporated milk and whiz, starting slowly and increasing the speed until the sauce is very smooth. Add the rest of the milk as you need it to keep the contents of the blender moving. When it is silky smooth, add the chicken stock, the pepper, salt, and spice mix and whiz until it's well mixed.

Start the pasta in a large kettle of boiling water. Cook for 11 to 12 minutes, drain, and keep warm.

Heat a sauté pan over medium high heat, pour in the lemon juice, and boil to reduce the amount of liquid by about half. When it is just bubbling over the bottom of the pan, drop the meat in to brown. Leave it to brown for 1 minute, then add the white parts of the onions. Don't stir until the lemon juice has disappeared, then add the pea pods. Deglaze the pan with the wine and continue cooking until the pea pods are heated through and crisp-tender, about 3 or 4 minutes. Pour the carrot sauce over the meat and vegetables and gently stir it in. Now add the drained pasta and stir again to mix. Cover and allow the dish to heat through for 3 to 5 minutes. When it's hot, toss in the green parts of the onions and mix through to give freshness to the dish.

To serve: Divide the pasta among 4 hot plates, dust with the Parmesan cheese, sprinkle with tomato strips, and enjoy!

Time Estimate: Preparation, 20 minutes; cooking, 6 minutes; unsupervised, 12 minutes

Nutritional Profile per Serving: Calories—298; % calories from fat—22%; fat (gm)—8 or 12% daily value; saturated fat (gm)—3; sodium (mg)—696; cholesterol (mg)—50; carbohydrates (gm)—36; dietary fiber (gm)—7; protein (gm)—23. Analysis includes suggested side dishes.

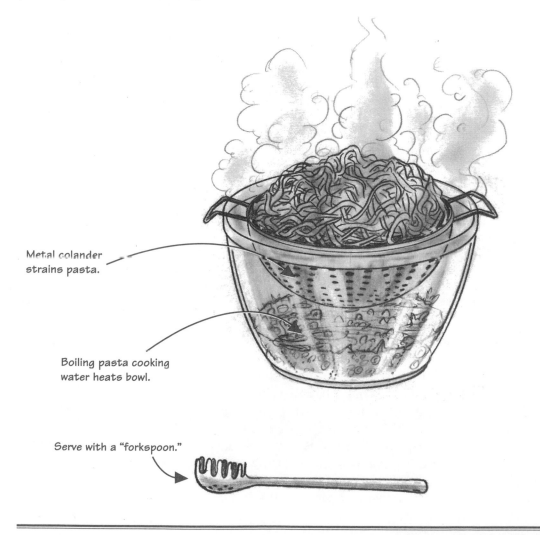

Metal colander strains pasta.

Boiling pasta cooking water heats bowl.

Serve with a "forkspoon."

The Skillet

Graham discovers he needs a better nonstick skillet.

There's nothing particularly earth-shattering about the idea that you'll need a skillet in a swift kitchen. What is important, however, is the material and design for a lasting nonstick surface.

I've always liked cast aluminum because it diffuses the heat so well. In the early 1990s the industry developed a method of taking an aluminum core and covering it in high-quality stainless steel. The surface was then treated to produce micropylons of stainless steel, like a defoliated forest which you need a microscope to see properly. Along came the plastics industry with a new polymer that was floated onto this stainless steel "forest," holding it in place and, for the first time, promising the sparkle of stainless, the heat spread of cast aluminum, and a nonstick surface that was built to last.

Several manufacturers have now added—quite literally—new *wrinkles* to the base. The pan base is indented so that up to 80 percent of the surface is out of the reach of the flashing naked steel spatula wielded by enthusiasts.

One of these designs uses a relative macro approach in what I call a *waffle* cut. This works very well and gives maximum surface protection but it also has a tremendous added benefit.

When meat or vegetable juices are driven out by direct heat, those juices evaporate and form a delicious crusty deposit on a plain metal pan. They do not form on an ordinary nonstick material but return to glaze the food which is being cooked. This is fine except for the fact that it's nice to have a pan glaze with which to create a very swift sauce by adding either stock or wine to deglaze the pan, thickening it with a little arrowroot and seasoning with fresh herbs. Bingo, you've got glistening, aromatic food in a jiffy! This is where the Steelon (Meyer Cookware) waffle cut comes in so handy. It traps the pan juices and acts like a small cauldron in which the juice evaporates and leaves a fine glaze. Using a small nylon or bamboo deglazer (see illustration) it is possible to create a perfectly flavored, nonfat, glistening sauce and have the benefits of a nonstick base which will last for years.

Nonstick Skillet

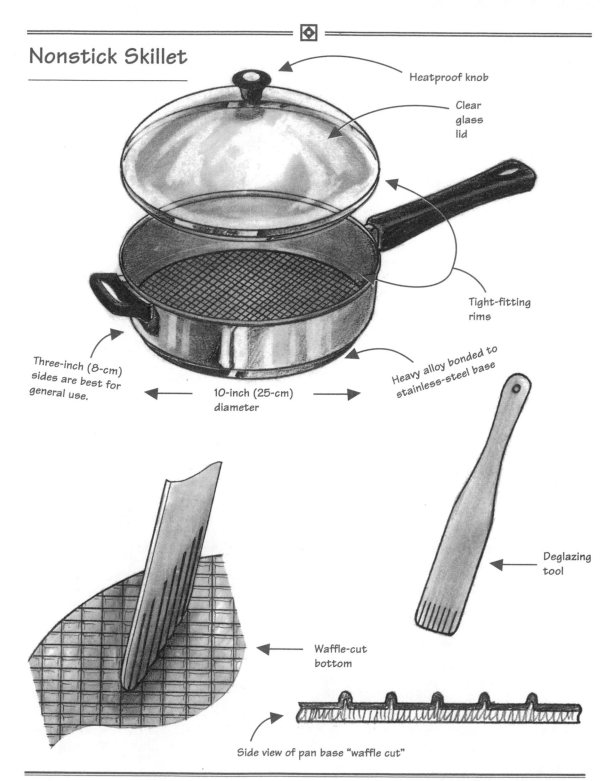

Heatproof knob

Clear glass lid

Tight-fitting rims

Three-inch (8-cm) sides are best for general use.

10-inch (25-cm) diameter

Heavy alloy bonded to stainless-steel base

Deglazing tool

Waffle-cut bottom

Side view of pan base "waffle cut"

Sautéed Turkey Breast with Fennel, Mushrooms, and Pears

Serves 4

2 large fennel bulbs
1/4 teaspoon ground allspice
1/4 teaspoon dried basil

Sauté

3 Bosc pears
2 cups de-alcoholized white zinfandel wine
1 tablespoon plus 1 (optional) teaspoon freshly squeezed lemon juice
2 teaspoons light olive oil with a dash of toasted sesame oil, divided
4 (6-inch or 15-cm) fennel stalks, trimmed and cut diagonally into 1/4-inch (.6-cm) slices
1 pound (454 gm) boneless, skinless turkey breast half
12 medium white mushrooms, cut into quarters (2 cups)
1/8 teaspoon salt
1/8 teaspoon freshly ground black pepper
1 tablespoon arrowroot mixed with 2 tablespoons de-alcoholized white zinfandel wine (slurry)
1/4 cup dried cranberries
1/4 teaspoon Hungarian paprika

Trim the stalks and stringy parts off the fennel bulbs, reserving the trim for later use. Cut the bulbs in half lengthwise, place on a steamer platform, and sprinkle with allspice and dried basil. Set aside to be steamed closer to serving time.

A sauté is rather like a stir-fry, so it's important to prepare each part before beginning to cook. Cut the tops and bottoms off the pears; peel, core, and cut the pears into eighths. Place all the trim (peelings and cores) in a medium-sized saucepan with the wine. Keep the pear pieces in a bowl of water with a tablespoon of lemon juice so they won't brown while you're waiting to use them. Save four 6-inch (15-cm) green fennel stalks and some of the "feathers" and toss the rest of the trim into the saucepan with the pear trim. Simmer while you prepare the rest of the ingredients. Cut the fennel stalks on the diagonal into 1/4-inch (.6-cm) pieces. Chop the fine feathery part to make 2 tablespoons.

Cut the turkey breast diagonally into 1/2-inch (.6-cm) slices across the grain of the meat. Start at the narrow end and cut the slices thinner as the breast gets wider. Three pieces will weigh 4 ounces (120 g) and there should be 12 of them. Preheat a large sauté pan and add 1 teaspoon of the oil. Drop the turkey pieces into the pan evenly over the bottom, sliding each piece so it catches the oil. Brown for 1 minute over high heat, then turn to brown the other side for another minute. Tip the turkey onto a plate and cover with a lid to keep warm. Pour the simmering wine through a sieve into the sauté pan and use it to "clean" the pan, making sure you get all the flavorful bits stuck to the bottom. Discard the strained trim. Pour the wine back into the saucepan and set aside to use in the sauce.

Heat water in the bottom of your steamer and start cooking the fennel bulbs now. Steam the fennel for 10 minutes.

Without washing the sauté pan, pour the remaining teaspoon of oil into it and heat over medium high heat. Fry the mushrooms, fennel stalks, and drained pear pieces for 4 minutes. Remove from the heat to stir in the salt, pepper, and the slurry. While it's still off the heat, add the turkey pieces, dried cranberries, and wine, stirring gently to mix well. Place over medium high heat just until the sauce begins to bubble. Sprinkle 1 teaspoon of the chopped fennel feathers and the Hungarian paprika over the top and taste. If it tastes too sweet, add the optional teaspoon of lemon juice.

To serve: Spoon the sauté onto plates with the fennel halves. Garnish with a sprinkling of fennel feathers and a dusting of paprika. I like a Baked Russet Potato half (page 166) and steamed Swiss Chard (page 158) with this dish.

Time Estimate: Preparation, 25 minutes; cooking, 21 minutes

Nutritional Profile per Serving: Calories—350; % calories from fat—22%; fat (gm)—8 or 13% daily value; saturated fat (gm)—2; sodium (mg)—423; cholesterol (mg)—52; carbohydrates (gm)—46; dietary fiber (gm)—11; protein (gm)—27. Analysis includes suggested side dishes.

The Food Processor

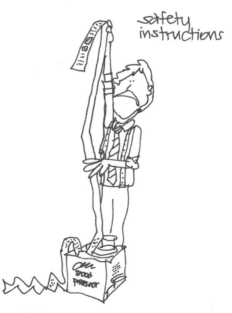

This is the breakthrough machine that almost jostles the blender off its perch on the kitchen counter. Many years ago, when it was first introduced, I had a very public struggle getting the lid both on and off, to say nothing of fitting the various blades. Totally exasperated, I literally hurled it aside and vowed never to let one darken my doorstep again! But life goes on and machines become more user friendly. So today I can finally stand up in public and, *almost* without looking down, I can operate a modern food processor . . . and boy is it *swift!*

Do I think it should be used from day to day? Well, I guess it depends upon the size of your family. Cooking for four is quite easy to do just using a knife. When four becomes more, and for special occasions and parties, a food processor is a real blessing.

safety instructions

The Food Processor

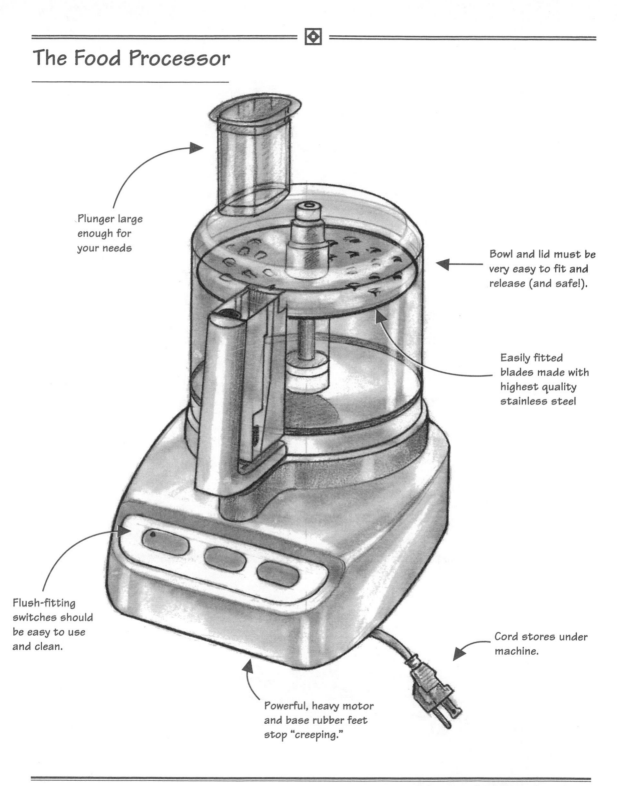

Plunger large enough for your needs

Bowl and lid must be very easy to fit and release (and safe!).

Easily fitted blades made with highest quality stainless steel

Flush-fitting switches should be easy to use and clean.

Cord stores under machine.

Powerful, heavy motor and base rubber feet stop "creeping."

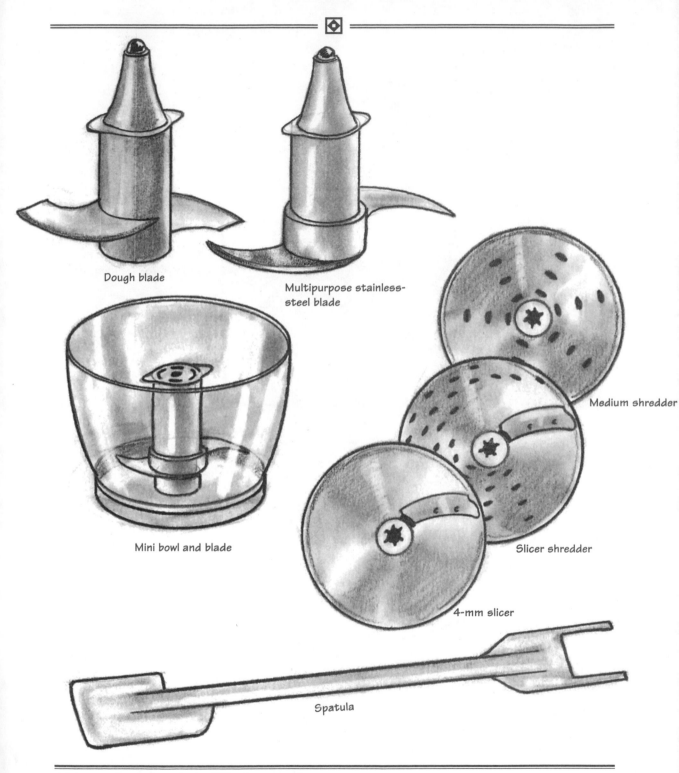

Dough blade

Multipurpose stainless-
steel blade

Mini bowl and blade

Medium shredder

Slicer shredder

4-mm slicer

Spatula

Turkey Meat Loaf

Serves 4

> I have found that onions chopped by machine or grated have a strong, bitter flavor. Therefore, I always chop, slice, or dice my onions by hand even though that might be a tearful process.

1 medium carrot
1 medium parsnip
1 teaspoon light olive oil with a dash of toasted sesame oil
2 cups finely chopped sweet onion
2 cloves garlic, peeled, bashed, and chopped
1/8 teaspoon salt
1/8 teaspoon freshly ground black pepper
8 ounces (227 gm) turkey thigh meat, trimmed of all fat and skin and cut into 2-inch (5-cm) chunks
8 ounces (227 gm) turkey breast meat, trimmed of all fat and skin and cut into 2-inch (5-cm) chunks

1/4 cup old-fashioned rolled oats
1½ teaspoons Scandinavia Ethmix (page 215)
1/4 cup egg substitute (I prefer Egg Beaters)

Sauce
1/4 cup yogurt cheese (page 210)
2 teaspoons Dijon mustard
1/4 teaspoon Scandinavia Ethmix
1/8 teaspoon ground red pepper (cayenne) (optional)

Preheat the oven to 350°F (180°C).

Cut the carrot and parsnip into 4-inch (10-cm) lengths to fit the feeder of your food processor. Grate on the larger-hole grating disk and set aside.

Heat a large, high-sided frying pan over medium high heat and add the oil. Fry the onions until they just begin to turn brown, about 4 minutes; then add the garlic and cook 1 minute more. Add the grated parsnip and carrot, salt, and pepper to the onions and continue cooking until tender, about 4 minutes.

Refit the processor with the cutting blade. Drop in the turkey pieces and pulse 20 times. Add the oats and pulse 15 more times, or until pretty well ground and mixed. Now add the cooked vegetables and 1½ teaspoons of the seasoning mix, and pulse another 10 times to thoroughly mix the ingredients. Pour in the egg substitute and pulse another 5 times to mix. Spray a 3¼ × 7¼ × 2½-inch (8 × 18 × 6-cm) loaf pan with cooking spray and fill with the meat mixture. Smooth the top with a wet spatula and bake for 30 minutes.

To make the sauce: Combine the yogurt, mustard, seasoning mix and cayenne.

To serve: Slice the meat loaf into 1/2-inch (1.25-cm) slices and lay them on a hot plate. Spoon a dollop of sauce on the side. I like the Grated Parsnips and Carrots (page 156) and Steamed Green Beans (page 150) served on the side.

Time Estimate: Preparation, 20 minutes; cooking, 9 minutes; unsupervised, 30 minutes

Nutritional Profile per Serving: Calories—469; % calories from fat—12%; fat (gm)—6 or 10% daily value; saturated fat (gm)—2; sodium (mg)—435; cholesterol (mg)—74; carbohydrates (gm)—72; dietary fiber (gm)—17; protein (gm)—36.   Analysis includes suggested side dishes.

Bison

I think that the best bison quote ever made was from Harold Danz, the executive director of the National Bison Association, when he said, "Animals that people eat do not become extinct. That's why we have so many more chickens than bald eagles in this country!"

The big problem for the bison came when the white man discovered that a tanned pelt could command $1,500 in London and that even when the market was oversupplied, the tongue of the mighty beast was so popular that it actually paid to kill an entire animal to harvest just its tongue. These not-so-charming excesses managed to decimate an estimated 60 million bison by the mid-nineteenth century, and by 1893, there were only between 300 and 1,000 bison remaining in the whole nation. The bounce-back has begun with an estimate of today's herds in the U.S. and Canada running at the 150,000 mark.

In many ways bison meat is very much like beef except denser and just a little bit sweeter. People who know their meats claim that once bison is savored, beef seems to pale slightly in comparison. What I like about it is that, as in the case of venison and ostrich, there are no growth hormones or antibiotics used. I'm also amazed at the difference between prime beef and bison from a fat/calories perspective. The meat can be cut into the same range of joints we find in beef cattle and cooked by similar methods in about the same time.

Nutritional Comparison of Meat
Based on 3-oz. cooked portions

	Bison	Beef Tenderloin	Chicken Breast	Pacific Salmon	Ostrich	Venison
Calories	122	179	140	153	108	134
Fat (gm)	2	9	3	9	2	3
Cholest. (mg)	70	71	72	56	66	95
Protein (gm)	24	24	26	17	22	26

What will be different for some time to come, apart from the nutritional benefits, is the price. You can expect to pay double the cost of beef, but you can make some economy by reducing the serving size by at least 25%. Because of bison meat's density, it shrinks less and satisfies more.

Buffalo Joe

Everyone raised in North America seems to have a Sloppy Joe in his or her gastronomic experience, and every recipe has its own secret ingredient. I've got several in this recipe, and they all add up to flavor with much less fat and refined carbohydrate. It's also a lot of fun and easy to fix!

> Try serving the Buffalo Joe over baked yams. I love this version and I think your family will like it too.

Serves 4

1½ teaspoons light olive oil with a dash of toasted sesame oil, divided
3/8 teaspoon salt, divided
3/8 teaspoon freshly ground black pepper, divided
8 ounces (224 gm) buffalo sirloin steak
1 medium onion, chopped
2 cloves garlic, peeled, bashed, and chopped
2 medium carrots, chopped
2 stalks celery, chopped
1 green bell pepper, seeded and chopped

16 medium mushrooms, chopped
1 teaspoon Greek Islands Ethmix (page 219)
1 tablespoon wild mushroom powder (optional)
1 cup no-salt-added tomato sauce
2 cups de-alcoholized Cabernet Sauvignon wine
1 teaspoon low-sodium tamari
1 tablespoon arrowroot mixed with 2 tablespoons de-alcoholized Cabernet Sauvignon (slurry)
4 whole wheat hamburger buns

Brush 1 teaspoon of the oil on a plate and sprinkle 1/8 teaspoon each of the salt and pepper over the oil. Rub the steak through the seasoned oil on both sides. Heat a large, high-sided skillet over high heat until it's very hot. Brown the meat for 2 minutes on each side and remove from the pan. Turn the heat down to medium, pour in the remaining oil, and cook the onion until it begins to wilt, about 2 minutes. Add the garlic, cook for 1 minute, then add the rest of the chopped vegetables. Sprinkle with the spice mix, the remaining 1/4 teaspoon salt, 1/4 teaspoon pepper, and the wild mushroom powder. Stir the seasonings into the vegetables and cook for 2 minutes.

Cut the browned meat into 2-inch (5-cm) chunks and drop into a food processor. Pulse a few times to chop the meat coarsely, as it is very tender and doesn't need to be finely ground. Add the chopped meat to the simmering vegetables and cook for 5 minutes. Pour in the tomato sauce, wine, tamari, and slurry, and bring back to a boil. Turn the heat down to simmer to keep warm. Toast the hamburger buns in a toaster or oven broiler.

To serve: Spoon the Buffalo Joe over the toasted buns on each of 4 hot plates. Arrange Steamed Mixed Greens (page 154) on the side.

Time Estimate: Preparation, 30 minutes; cooking, 20 minutes

Nutritional Profile per Serving: Calories—269; % calories from fat—13%; fat (gm)—4 or 6% daily value; saturated fat (gm)—1; sodium (mg)—548; cholesterol (mg)—46; carbohydrates (gm)—40; dietary fiber (gm)—9; protein (gm)—23. Analysis includes suggested side dishes.

Drip Stew

An old idea whose time has yet to come?

One of the world's earliest known cooking vessels was a clay pot made with three hollow legs. The legs were filled with water and then dug into the cinders of a hot fire.

The water boiled, the steam filled the covered vessel and cooked the food—a simple and elegant idea about 50,000 years old.

I adapted this for a possible future modern appliance somewhat like a Crock-Pot, yet more similar to the ancient Chinese vessel.

In this case, the water boils around the outside and up into an inside core of a widely available German cake pan called a kugelhopf pan. It fits neatly into a 6½-quart pan with a close-fitting lid.

The water turns into steam, rises, and condenses on the lid. It then drips down onto quite tough, inexpensive cuts of meat to create a perfect stew. The meat and vegetables cook by indirect 200°F heat, an ideal temperature for tenderizing these tough but flavorful cuts.

Best of all, seasonings such as curry, chili, or Moroccan (see page 218) are perfectly absorbed to become a part of the whole dish. It does take time to cook, but much less time to prepare. So, slowly, swiftly does it!

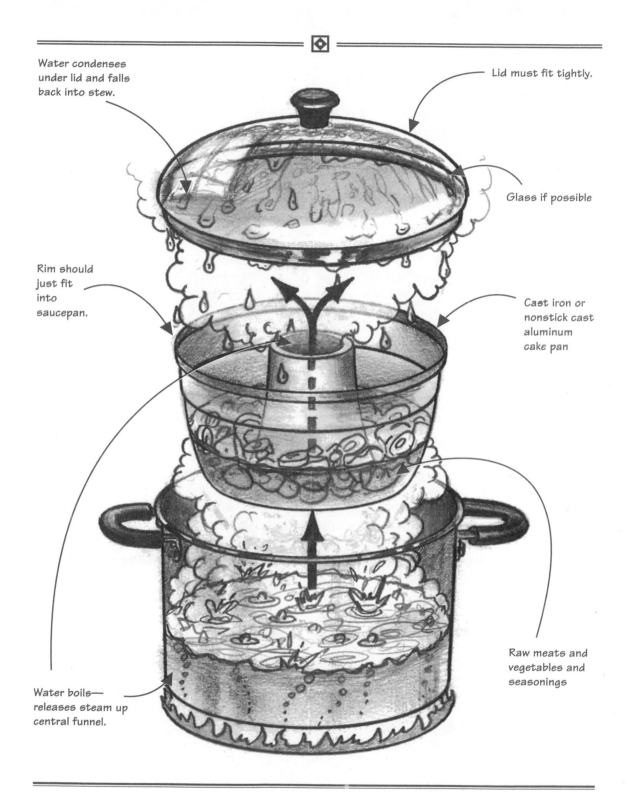

Water condenses under lid and falls back into stew.

Lid must fit tightly.

Glass if possible

Rim should just fit into saucepan.

Cast iron or nonstick cast aluminum cake pan

Water boils—releases steam up central funnel.

Raw meats and vegetables and seasonings

Lamb Vegetable Curry

There is no liquid added to this stew. Pan juices are created from the cooking food and condensation from the lid. The flavors are very concentrated while the color remains bright and the textures distinctive.

Serves 6

1 pound (450 gm) lamb shoulder, trimmed of all
    fat and cut into 1-inch (2.5-cm) pieces
1/2 cup roughly chopped onion
3 gloves garlic, peeled, bashed, and chopped
1 pound (450 gm) carrots, peeled and cut
    into 1-inch (2.5-cm) pieces
4 medium red potatoes, peeled and quartered lengthwise
1/2 teaspoon salt, divided
1/4 teaspoon freshly ground black pepper
2 tablespoons India Ethmix (page 218)
    or good Madras curry powder

2 cups frozen green peas, thawed
2 cups fresh mushrooms, cut in quarters
2 tablespoons chopped Major Grey mango chutney
2 tablespoons arrowroot mixed with
    1/4 cup Chardonnay wine (slurry)
1/2 cup yogurt cheese (page 210)

Garnish
1 tablespoon chopped fresh mint or cilantro

Combine the lamb and the vegetables in a large bowl. Sprinkle 1/4 teaspoon of the salt, the pepper, and the seasoning mix over all and toss to coat. Place the mixture in a Bundt or kugelhopf pan and set in a large Dutch oven. Pour enough boiling water into the Dutch oven to come halfway up the side of the pan. Cover and simmer 1 hour or until everything is tender.

Strain the cooking liquid into a small saucepan. Tip the meat and vegetables into a large, high-sided skillet and stir in the peas, mushrooms, and chutney. Cover to retain the heat.

Pour the slurry into the pan juices in the saucepan. Heat over medium high heat, stirring with a wire whisk until the sauce clears and thickens. Add the remaining salt. Place the yogurt cheese in a large measuring cup. Pour a little of the hot thickened sauce into the yogurt and whisk until smooth. Pour the rest of the sauce into the yogurt slowly, stirring as you pour.

Add the sauce to the meat and vegetables in the skillet and place over medium heat just until heated through. (Do not allow to boil or the sauce will curdle.) Sprinkle with mint or cilantro and serve.

Time Estimate: Preparation, 25 minutes; cooking, 5 minutes; unsupervised, 1 hour

Nutritional Profile per Serving: Calories—407; % calories from fat—25%; fat (gm)—12 or 18% daily value; saturated fat (gm)—4; sodium (mg)—282; cholesterol (mg)—91; carbohydrates (gm)—43; dietary fiber (gm)—8; protein (gm)—33

Pork Tenderloin on a Cedar Plank with Apples and Onions

You'll find an illustrated discussion of the cedar plank on page 52. This recipe can also be very successfully made in a small baking pan.

Serves 4

1 teaspoon light olive oil with a dash of toasted sesame oil
2 onions, peeled and sliced lengthwise
2 cooking apples (Jonagold, Gravenstein, Winesap), peeled and sliced
1 cup chopped red bell pepper
1 teaspoon caraway seeds

1¼ teaspoons Poland Ethmix (page 217), divided
1/4 teaspoon salt
1/4 teaspoon freshly ground black pepper
1 pound (454 gm) pork tenderloin
1 tablespoon chopped parsley

Preheat the oven to 350°F (180°C). Heat the oil in a high-sided skillet over medium high heat. Add the onions and cook, stirring often, for a full 5 minutes. The more you cook down strong onions, the sweeter they become. Toss in the apple slices, chopped bell pepper, caraway seeds, 1 teaspoon of the spice mix, the salt and black pepper. Reduce the heat to medium and continue cooking for 10 to 15 minutes or until the apples and onions are very tender.

Preheat the cedar baking plank in the preheated oven for 15 minutes. Trim any fat or tough white tissue from the outside of the pork tenderloin. Cut about 3/4 of the way through the roast lengthwise and spread the sides apart. Pound gently with your fist to make a flat piece of meat. Dust both sides very lightly with salt, pepper, and the remaining 1/4 teaspoon of spice mix.

Lay the meat on the hot plank and spread the apples and onions over the top. Bake for 30 minutes. The meat will be done at this point, 150°F (65°C) internally, but it will look pink because it's been buried in apples and onions. Heat a nonstick frying pan and brown it quickly on both sides to improve its appearance. It will remain tender and succulent if you give it a quick 1 or 2 minutes per side.

To serve: Divide the vegetables among 4 hot plates. Slice the roast on the diagonal into 12 pieces and lay 3 pieces on each bed of vegetables. I like to serve Steamed Baby Carrots (page 152) and Steamed Tiny Red Potatoes (page 162) on the side. Dust all over with parsley mixed with 1/4 teaspoon spice mix.

Time Estimate: Preparation, 20 minutes; cooking, 20 minutes; unsupervised, 20 minutes

Nutritional Profile per Serving: Calories—418; % calories from fat—22%; fat (gm)—10 or 16% daily value; saturated fat (gm)—3; sodium (mg)—294; cholesterol (mg)—68; carbohydrates (gm)—54; dietary fiber (gm)—9; protein (gm)—30. Analysis includes suggested side dishes.

The Stir-Fry

By tradition, the pan of preference for stir-frying is the wok, a bowl of beaten steel with two handles—simple and *somewhat* swift. It's only *somewhat* swift because the wok lacks convenience in the domestic kitchen. It isn't easy, especially on an electric stovetop.

Because of these drawbacks, we've been treated to wok-sided but flat-based pans. The walls in these pans remain relatively cool. Their shape, while nodding to tradition, actually reduces the amount of food that can be properly stir-fried on a domestic stovetop.

My choice is to get a pan of about 10 inches in diameter, the largest practical size for current electric elements, and at least 3 inches deep, with straight sides. The base should be very well designed to diffuse the heat and the interior should be non-stick. My personal preference runs to the textured or patterned base so that a glaze can form to reinforce a simple swift sauce (please see "The Skillet" on page 94).

Again, I do appreciate that it does not look like a wok but I can assure you that it will be much easier to use on your home stove.

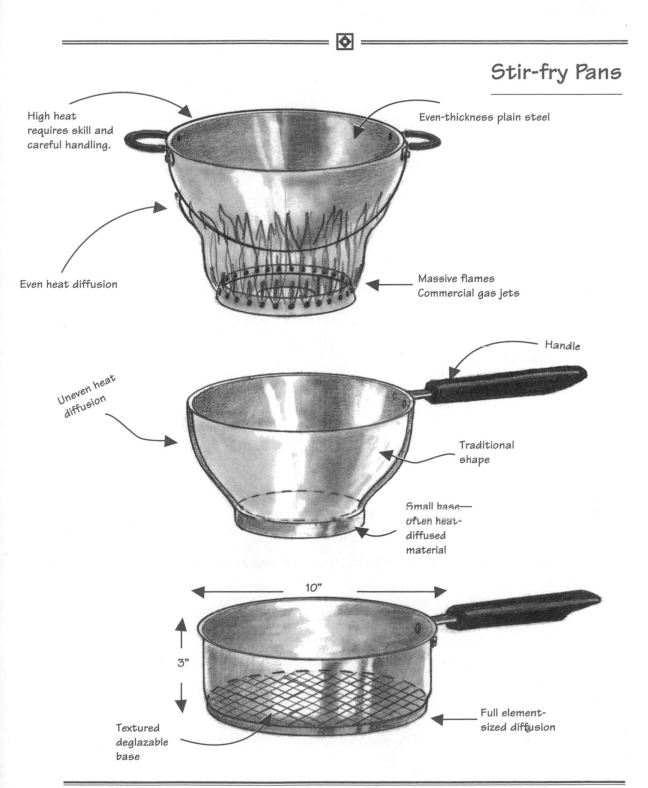

High heat requires skill and careful handling.

Even-thickness plain steel

Even heat diffusion

Massive flames Commercial gas jets

Handle

Uneven heat diffusion

Traditional shape

Small base— often heat-diffused material

10"

3"

Textured deglazable base

Full element-sized diffusion

Stir-Fried Pork with Pea Pods and Baby Corn

Serves 4

12 green onions

1 teaspoon light olive oil with a dash of toasted sesame oil, divided

2 star anise

2 large cloves garlic, peeled, bashed, and chopped

10 dime-sized slices fresh gingerroot, finely chopped

8 ounces (250 gm) pork tenderloin, trimmed and sliced into 1/4-inch (.75-cm) slices

1/16 teaspoon salt

1/16 teaspoon freshly ground black pepper

2 large red bell peppers, cored and cut into 1/2-inch (1.5-cm) strips, 2 inches (6 cm) long

4 ounces (100 gm) fresh sugar snap peas, tips and strings removed

4 ounces (100 gm) canned baby corncobs

1 tablespoon cornstarch

1 cup de-alcoholized Chardonnay wine

3 tablespoons low-sodium tamari sauce

1/2 teaspoon toasted sesame oil

1/4 teaspoon Shanghai Coastline Ethmix (page 215)

Cut the white parts of the green onions into 1/4-inch (.75-cm) slices. Cut the green parts into 2-inch (5-cm) strips and reserve for later. Heat a high-sided skillet over medium heat. Add 1/2 teaspoon of the oil, the star anise, garlic, ginger, and the white part of the onions. Stir-fry over medium heat briefly, just to release the volatile oils, being careful not to scorch the garlic and onion. Transfer this flavoring mix or *bao syang* to a bowl, discarding the star anise. Heat the remaining 1/2 teaspoon of oil in the same skillet over medium high heat. Drop the pork slices evenly over the bottom of the pan and resist the urge to stir them until they are well and truly browned on one side, about 2½ minutes. Lightly dust with salt and pepper. Turn over and cook for about 30 seconds on high heat. Add the reserved *bao syang* mixture, the red pepper strips, green parts of the onions, sugar snap peas, and baby corncobs, turning and tossing to stir-fry for about 1 minute.

To make the sauce: In a small bowl, combine the cornstarch with the wine and tamari and pour into the pan with the meat and vegetables. Cook for 30 seconds or until clear and glossy. Add the sesame oil and spice mix, stirring to mix and coat.

To serve: Spoon the stir-fry onto 4 hot plates with a slotted spoon and divide the sauce among 4 tiny bowls to serve alongside. Serve Steamed Pearl Rice (page 163) in individual bowls set on each plate.

Time Estimate: Preparation, 25 minutes; cooking, 26 minutes

> *Bao syang* means "an explosion of fragrance" in Chinese cooking. Fresh gingerroot, fresh garlic, and green onions thrown into hot oil are the most commonly used ingredients. I can get the same burst of aroma with just 1/2 teaspoon of oil. In this recipe, I have added star anise to the more common threesome.

Nutritional Profile per Serving: Calories—336; % calories from fat—17%; fat (gm)—6 or 10% daily value; saturated fat (gm)—2; sodium (mg)—734; cholesterol (mg)—34; carbohydrates (gm)—48; dietary fiber (gm)—4; protein (gm)—20. Analysis includes suggested side dishes.

Venison

Once again . . . the term *swift* which I'm using for this book is a combination of the short time it takes to put food on the table and its essentially beneficial nutritive values. Both must be achieved so as not to damage the pleasure of eating. Pleasure depends, of course, on the palate of the consumer. The essential gaminess of venison is often paired with a robust red wine and juniper berry marinade, but if this doesn't appeal to your taste, never fear. Things have changed since Robin Hood invaded the king's lands in search of forbidden flesh.

Deer farms are springing up all over the world in order to meet the demand for red meat that is low in fat, has flavor, is given no hormone treatment, and includes swift cooking times.

Recently a farmer in New Zealand coined a new word to draw a clear distinction between the unpredictable wild meat of the past and the uniformly mild, tender, vacuum-packed cuts of today. That term is *Cervena*, which owes its source to the Latin *cervidae*, meaning "deer," and the English word *venison*, which originally meant "hunting." Since it is a trademarked name it is hard to imagine that it would take the place of the word *venison* on the menu, but it could be a qualification, as in Cervena venison. That would guarantee a consistency that might otherwise be missing.

Deer meat is dark red with very little fat. The smaller the deer, the more tender; the larger the animal, the coarser the meat. Where so little fat is present the meat needs to be cooked swiftly and done to the 140°F mark on a meat thermometer when dealing with tender cuts and, of course, braised or stewed for the tougher cuts. The Cervena folk recommend 425°F oven temperatures for their roasts—allowing 3½ minutes for each ½ inch (1 cm) of meat thickness. This is done to seal in the juices. I prefer 350°F in my convection oven (page 70) and five minutes per ½ inch (1 cm). When grilling, allow 2 minutes on either side for 1 inch (2 cm) and only 1 minute on either side for a swift sauté.

The most tender roasts and steaks come from the hind leg saddle cuts. Desinewed shoulder cuts are quite tender, too. Shoulder meat, forequarter, and leg trimmings are best for ground meat and stews. The most tender luxury cuts are what you're apt to find in the frozen food section of your local market.

Now here's the comparison list of low-fat meats to let you see what's in it for you.

I don't think that venison is quite done yet, graham.

Nutritional Comparison of Meat

Based on 3-oz. cooked portions

	Venison	Beef Tenderloin	Chicken Breast	Pacific Salmon	Ostrich	Bison
Calories	134	179	140	153	108	122
Fat (gm)	3	9	3	9	2	2
Cholest. (mg)	95	71	72	56	66	70
Protein (gm)	26	24	26	17	22	24

Rack of Venison with
Wild Mushroom-Currant Jelly Sauce

Serves 8

2 teaspoons flour
1 teaspoon Germany Ethmix (page 217)
1/8 teaspoon salt
3-pound (1.36-kg) rack of venison

Sauce
.35 ounce (10 gm) packet dried wild mushrooms
1 cup boiling water
2 tablespoons red currant jelly
1 tablespoon balsamic vinegar
1/4 cup mushroom water
1/2 teaspoon arrowroot mixed with
    1 teaspoon mushroom water (slurry)

Preheat the oven to 350°F (180°C).

Combine the flour, spice mix, and salt. Place the venison in a large resealable plastic bag and sprinkle the spice and flour mixture over the top. Close the bag and shake until the whole roast has a light dusting of flour on it. Remove the roast from the bag and lay it on a rack in a roasting pan.

Set the roast in the preheated oven. Bake for 30 minutes or until an instant-read meat thermometer reaches 140°F (60°C). The roast should be pink in the middle. Let it rest for 10 minutes before carving.

To make the sauce: Drop the dried mushrooms into the boiling water and soak, off the heat, for 30 minutes. Drain the water from the mushrooms through a fine sieve into a small saucepan. Reduce the water by half over high heat and set aside. Cut the mushrooms into fine strips. Place the mushroom strips in a small sauté pan over low heat and stir in the currant jelly. Continue stirring until the jelly liquefies, then add the balsamic vinegar and 1/4 cup of the mushroom water, saving the rest for other sauces or soups. Pull the pan from the heat, add the slurry, and return to the heat to thicken and clear.

To serve: Carve the roast into 8 small chops and lay one on each of 8 hot plates. Spoon some sauce on each. I like to serve Swift Roasted Sweet Potato Spears (page 167) across each other next to the meat and Steamed Cauliflower (page 153) as a side vegetable.

Time Estimate: Preparation, 30 minutes; cooking, 36 minutes; unsupervised, 40 minutes

---

Nutritional Profile per Serving: Calories—218; % calories from fat—25%; fat (gm)—6 or 9% daily value; saturated fat (gm)—2; sodium (mg)—426; cholesterol (mg)—61; carbohydrates (gm)—22; dietary fiber (gm)—4; protein (gm)—20. Analysis includes suggested side dishes.

Meatless Entrees

Mainly Meatless and the MEV

we owe it all to protein!!

For several years now I've suggested that you might like to look at what I call *meat in the minor key*. There is really no point in being legalistic and demanding of meat eaters. Nobody likes to be told to *stop* doing something. We usually respond better to a gradual decrease, *provided* we have a reason to change and the hope of a definite benefit. I've noticed that a common question is always asked: "Will I get enough protein for strength or energy?" Well, let's look at this from the serving-size perspective and see.

Flesh-based protein has its side effects largely because it usually packs fat. Looking at a 2,000-calorie-a-day total, our adult protein need comes in at about 60 grams per day.

I've come to look upon protein as a two-strand necklace with one strand having nine pearls and the other thirteen pearls. Each "pearl" represents one of the twenty-two amino acids that make up a complete protein. This necklace is only complete when both are worn together. The amino acids in the first loop are called essential because the body can't produce them the way an oyster assembles the pearl from within. The second string can be synthesized by the body.

Somehow we've swallowed the idea that you can *only* get a complete protein "necklace" from living creatures, especially from slabs of good red beef. We seem to believe that a complete protein only comes in *one* unit, like an egg. Whilst plant proteins may lack one or more of these amino acid "pearls," it doesn't mean that vegetables are incomplete. We now know that when we match certain plants, we can get complete necklaces of protein without any flesh protein.

This is how it happens. Visualize three overlapping circles, one of which is quite small.

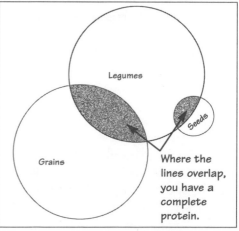

Where the lines overlap, you have a complete protein.

Now insert *grains* and *legumes* on the two large circles and *seeds* on the smallest circle. At each point that the circles overlap there is a complete protein; for example, rice and beans, which form the basis for many classic Caribbean dishes. The areas where the lines don't overlap are less likely to have a complete "two-string" twenty-two-pearl protein.

Here are some nondairy examples of complete proteins:

- Great Northern beans (small white) and rye bread
- Black-eyed peas and cornbread
- Tofu (see page 126 for low-fat types) and rice
- Kidney beans and rice
- Black beans and whole wheat pita
- Peanut butter and whole wheat bread
- Corn tortillas and pinto beans

In the USA we appear to be consuming up to three times more animal protein than we need...

At present, in the U.S.A., we appear to be consuming up to three times more animal protein than we need. This is being stored as fat, as is all excessive consumption (when it exceeds our daily caloric output). A mainly meatless menu can bring the protein levels into line with our real need and help to reduce cholesterol levels (in some cases substantially), especially when accompanied by the other connected lifestyle changes.

A brief note here about the fiber that comes along for the ride in all whole fruits and vegetables. Fiber can provide two important benefits. Soluble fiber helps to reduce cholesterol in your blood; the result is that your LDL (low-density lipoprotein) cholesterol is lowered. Blood sugars can also be lowered, which may be helpful to those with diabetes and/or hypoglycemia. Insoluble fibers move into the digestive track and soften the passage and elimination of food we eat. The result is a better and swifter evacuation of solids with multiple health benefits.

For example, people who consume high-fiber diets experience lower cancer risk than those with low-fiber diets.

Quite properly you should ask, "Are my loved ones and I getting enough protein and fiber?" My answer is, in these recipes, YES! And to help you measure my words, here is an equation to find out what your and your loved ones' real needs are for protein.

Each adult needs 0.8 grams of protein daily for every kilogram of body weight (1 kilogram equals 2.2 pounds). In my case, I weigh 201 pounds (x 2.2=91 kilograms x 0.8=73 grams of protein required daily). My wife, Treena, weighs 138 pounds (x 2.2=62 kilograms x 0.8=50 grams of protein required daily).

In your case, you weigh _____ pounds (divided by 2.2) equals _____ kilograms (× 0.8) equals _____ grams protein. To get a rough-but-ready idea of how much you need, consider that 1 ounce of meat, fish, poultry, or cheese equals 7 grams of protein; 1/2 cup of cooked lentils, dried beans, or peas equals 8 grams of protein; 1 cup of cooked cereal with milk equals 10 grams of protein; and 1 slice of bread equals 3 grams of protein per ounce.

Now just think about it—you don't have to keep totals and get bothered. What I need you to do is to see how easy it is to get enough protein from a lifestyle of meat in the minor key and/or the adoption of a meatless menu several times a month.

Just by highlighting some of the foods in one simple day's menu you can get a very swift idea of its protein content. As an example:

Breakfast	3/4 cup cereal with 1 cup skim milk	3–8 grams
	2 slices toast/muffin (4 oz.)	6 grams
Lunch	2 bread slices (sandwich)	6 grams
	1 oz. low-fat cheese	7 grams
Dinner	3 oz. chicken breast (or beans & tortilla)	21 grams
	1/2 cup peas	4 grams
	1/2 cup yogurt	4 grams
	TOTAL	**51–56 grams**

This protein intake is sufficient for me and about 17 grams more than Treena needs. If you replace the chicken breast with one of my MEV recipes, the result is usually just right.

Because of this, I've devoted a major part of this book to the introduction of the MEV (an acronym for Molded Ethnic Vegetables).

The traditional meat eater's plate is divided into three, with the meat being the focus of the plate:

A veal chop dominates the plate; the vegetable is used as garnish.

A well-balanced meat eater's plate is divided into what is called the "rule of five." In other words, the plate can be divided into equal 20 percent segments:

Though smaller, the chop is still the focus.

In this illustration we see equal-sized portions of four vegetables and one meat. In this example, by tradition the veal chop is the focus. The chop costs up to ten times as much as the vegetables and commands star billing on the menu. We usually order by flesh protein, not vegetable garnish.

This is why, in my opinion, we don't get quite the same enjoyment from a meatless plate where the veal is replaced by bok choy, for instance, and all is served in one giant, level plateful. *There is no focus!*

This is where the MEV comes into its own. Just take the veal chop off the plate and replace it with a cork-shaped cylinder measuring 3 inches (7.5 cm) in diameter, and 4 inches (10 cm) in height, holding about 9 ounces (252 g) of layered vegetable flavors. *Now you have the focus back*! And even more so, because it packs more flavor, more color, more texture, and more aroma than any single flesh portion can possibly provide.

I'm having trouble focusing...

I liken the MEV to chocolates—the kind with a surprising, creative center (that I *used* to sample)! Break through the thin shell and the center spills into your mouth, full of smooth cherry liqueur, crisp caramelized almonds, or fudged espresso coffee, always a surprise, always surpassing the plainly predictable piece of dark chocolate.

So it is with the MEV, because the mold is first lined

When the chop is replaced with another vegetable, the plate lacks a point of reference and seems flat.

MEVs like chocolates

with a moist, colorful shell like blanched bright green leaves or roasted red or yellow sweet peppers or orange-colored squash. The center is then developed using an international starch as the binder—foods like the plump Italian arborio rice, or the tiny pasta-like couscous from North Africa, or the sweet seedlike grain quinoa from South America, the pinto bean of Mexico, the black beans of Colombia, or the black-eyed peas of the Deep Southern American kitchen.

Wherever those starches set the scene, the *swift seasonings* should follow. The Ethmix blends provide regional flavors enjoyed for thousands of years of written culinary history. India, for example, has its incredible diversity of spiced combinations, and Australia boasts its new-wave *bush tucker* flavors. Swirled into the midst of these flavored starches are the textures of mushroom, sweet corn, dates, pistachio or pine nuts, each of which comes from the cuisine of the microculture you've selected to creatively reproduce.

The MEV lifts up a multilayered and flavored focus for the vegetable-only platter.

Now, take these flavors along with wine, stock, or broth, whiz up a blender sauce in a flash, and heat—ready to serve.

It's all so *easy* and such *fun* and it can be done ahead of time. The MEV is easily reheated in the special mold set I've designed. This will help you be delighted with the result, but if you can't locate the mold, don't give up. Try using a 10-ounce cup, a small bowl, or a tin can that holds about the same volume and set them on a cookie sheet.

Best of all, the MEV can provide a very important *variety* to your meals as it celebrates the wide world of vegetables and seasonings and confirms that meatless meals can be part of your weekly menu.

The MEV Molds

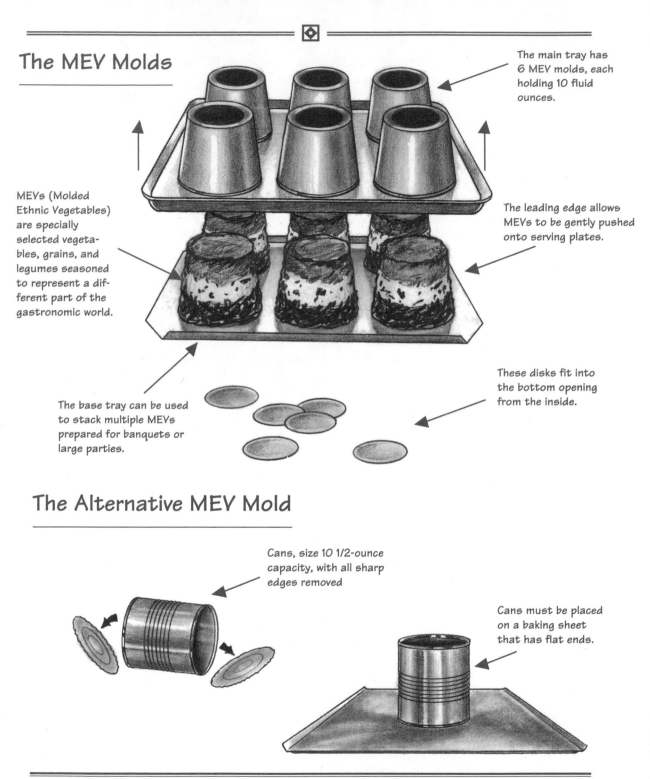

The main tray has 6 MEV molds, each holding 10 fluid ounces.

MEVs (Molded Ethnic Vegetables) are specially selected vegetables, grains, and legumes seasoned to represent a different part of the gastronomic world.

The leading edge allows MEVs to be gently pushed onto serving plates.

The base tray can be used to stack multiple MEVs prepared for banquets or large parties.

These disks fit into the bottom opening from the inside.

The Alternative MEV Mold

Cans, size 10 1/2-ounce capacity, with all sharp edges removed

Cans must be placed on a baking sheet that has flat ends.

Sweet Potato, Mushroom, and Pea MEV with a Mint Sauce

Serves 4

2 pounds (908 gm) sweet potatoes, halved
1 (.35-ounce or 10-gm) packet dried wild mushrooms
1 cup boiling water
1 tablespoon toasted pine nuts
2 cups frozen petit peas, thawed
1/4 teaspoon grated nutmeg
4 teaspoons mint sauce (see note to make your own, or Crosse & Blackwell makes a nice one)

Preheat the oven to 450°F (230°C). Bake the sweet potato halves for 15 minutes for small ones or up to 30 minutes for larger ones. Drop the dried mushrooms into the boiling water and let soak for at least 30 minutes. Peel the sweet potatoes when they're cool enough to handle and mash with a fork. Drain the mushrooms, saving the flavorful water for other dishes, and cut into thin strips. Combine the pine nuts, mushrooms, peas, and nutmeg with the sweet potatoes and stir to mix.

Spray 4 MEV or other 1-cup molds with vegetable oil cooking spray and the sweet potato mixture. Press into the mold or container firmly. Reduce the oven heat to 350°F (175°C) and bake 20 minutes. Serve with the mint sauce. Steamed Cauliflower (page 153) is an appropriate side dish.

Mint Sauce
Makes 1/2 cup, or 4–6 servings

3 tablespoons confectioners' sugar
3 tablespoons water
1/4 cup malt vinegar
1/4 cup chopped mint leaves

Combine the sugar and water in a small saucepan and heat just enough to dissolve the sugar. Off the heat, pour in the vinegar and mint leaves and allow to stand for at least 1/2 hour. Strain into a small bowl and serve. If you don't use it all, store in the refrigerator.

Nutritional Profile per Serving: Calories—19; % calories from fat—0%; fat (gm)—0 or 0% daily value; saturated fat (gm)—0; sodium (mg)—0; cholesterol (mg)—0; carbohydrates (gm)—5; dietary fiber (gm)—0; protein (gm)—0

Time Estimate: Preparation, 15 minutes; cooking, 30 minutes; unsupervised, 20 minutes

---

Nutritional Profile per Serving: Calories—365; % calories from fat—8%; fat (gm)—3 or 5% daily value; saturated fat (gm)—0; sodium (mg)—167; cholesterol (mg)—0; carbohydrates (gm)—77; dietary fiber (gm)—13; protein (gm)—11. Analysis includes suggested side dishes.

Winter Squash with Black Bean Salsa MEV

Save this recipe for the fall and winter when the squash has had time to develop flavor and sweetness.

Serves 4

4 acorn squash, halved and seeds removed
1 teaspoon light olive oil with a dash of toasted sesame oil
1 cup chopped onion
1 cup chopped red bell pepper
1 serrano chili, finely chopped (include the seeds if you like it hot)
5 sun-dried tomatoes, finely chopped
1/2 cup frozen corn kernels
1 (15-ounce or 425-gm) can low-salt black beans, drained and rinsed
1/4 teaspoon ground red pepper (cayenne)
1 tablespoon freshly squeezed lime juice
1 tablespoon chopped fresh cilantro
1/4 teaspoon salt

Sauce
1 cup mashed squash
3/4 cup evaporated skim milk
1/4 teaspoon ground white pepper
1/4 teaspoon ground cumin
1 tablespoon freshly squeezed lime juice

Garnish
2 tablespoons chopped fresh cilantro

Preheat the oven to 350°F (180°C). Put the squash halves, skin side up, on a rack in a roasting pan and bake for 40 minutes or until very soft. Set aside to cool.

Heat the oil in a high–sided skillet over medium high heat. Fry the onion, stirring often so it won't scorch, for about 3 minutes or until it becomes translucent. Add the red bell pepper, serranos, and dried tomatoes; stir and cook for another 3 minutes. Stir in the corn, beans, cayenne pepper, lime juice, cilantro, and salt. Set the salsa aside while you prepare the molds.

Peel the baked squash and discard the peelings. Mash the squash with a potato masher and reserve 1 cup for the sauce. Spray 4 MEV molds or other 1–cup molds with vegetable oil cooking spray. Scoop squash into each mold and press to cover the bottom and all the way up the sides, saving enough for the top. Divide the salsa among the 4 molds and press down. Cover the top with the rest of the mashed squash and press down gently. Bake in the preheated oven for 20 minutes to heat through.

Place the reserved squash in a blender and whiz, using just enough of the evaporated milk to keep it moving. When it is very smooth, add the rest of the milk, the white pepper, cumin, and lime juice and whiz just to mix. Pour into a small saucepan and place over medium heat until heated through.

To serve: Unmold each MEV onto a hot dinner plate, pour sauce around the edges, and sprinkle some chopped cilantro over the top. Serve with Steamed Mixed Greens (page 154) alongside.

Time Estimate: Preparation, 25 minutes; cooking, 6 minutes; unsupervised, 60 minutes

Nutritional Profile per Serving: Calories—378; % calories from fat 6%; fat (gm)—2 or 4% daily value; saturated fat (gm)—0; sodium (mg)—747; cholesterol (mg)—2; carbohydrates (gm)—87; dietary fiber (gm)—25; protein (gm)—17. Analysis includes suggested side dishes.

Tofu

regarding Tofu with suspicion...

In its traditional form, tofu is simply our commonly grown soybean ground up between granite wheels and boiled to release its milklike substance. To this is added one of the classic solidifiers, either a salt or an acid; then the curd is gently pressed to produce a soft, medium, or quite firm product. After thousands of years, low-fat engineers have discovered tofu and begun to prepare it in uniquely convenient packages.

One company, Morinaga Nutritional Foods, Inc., has delivered a soy tofu that is actually made in a pouch that is sealed *before* it is made and remains "fresh" for up to ten months! It is shelf stable, has no preservatives, is low in sodium, and has only 1 gram of fat per serving. You may call 1–800–NOW–TOFU to find out where to get it in your area.

So, now let's look at some of the numbers:

100-gram serving size	Calories	Total Fat gm	Cholesterol mg	Sodium mg	Protein gm	Carbohydrates gm
Breast of Chicken, skinless	165	4	77	70	30	0
Tofu 4% fat (traditional)	152	10	0	13	16	4
Mori-Nu 1% fat (retort pack)	41	1	0	94	7	1

The extremely low cost of tofu as a competitive protein and its brand-new container makes it worth considering as part of a package of low-fat protein. Since my work involves discovering how to find *variety on the lighter side* rather than making substitutions, it follows that I must give a good deal of attention to this as an important "future" food.

Peruvian Tofu and Vegetables

Serves 4

- 1 teaspoon light olive oil with a dash of toasted sesame oil
- 1 medium onion, cut into 1/2-inch (1.75-cm) dice
- 3 cloves garlic, peeled, bashed, and chopped
- 3 tablespoons low-sodium tomato paste
- 1 cup de-alcoholized red wine
- 4 medium yellow Finn potatoes, cut in 1/2-inch (1.75-cm) dice (2 generous cups)
- 3 carrots, peeled and cut in 1/2-inch (1.75-cm) dice (1½ generous cups)
- 1 (14½ -ounce or 411-gm) can no-salt-added diced tomatoes in juice
- 1 pound (454 gm) 1% tofu, cut in 1-inch (2.5-cm) cubes
- 12 kalamata olives, halved and pitted
- 2 heaping teaspoons capers
- 1 cup low-sodium vegetable stock (page 210)
- 2 bay leaves
- 1/4 teaspoon ground red pepper (cayenne)
- 1/4 teaspoon ground allspice
- 1/4 teaspoon salt
- 2 cups thickly sliced mushrooms
- 1 cup frozen petit peas
- 1 teaspoon arrowroot mixed with 2 teaspoons de-alcoholized red wine (slurry)

> Capers seem to come in bottles with openings too narrow to get a measuring spoon into. What I do is pour the whole bottle into a measuring cup, take out what I need, then pour the rest back. This way I don't lose the brine, which keeps capers from "going off."

Put the oil in a large high-sided skillet over medium high heat. Fry the onion for 2 minutes or until it starts to wilt and color. Add the garlic and tomato paste. Reduce the heat to medium and stir until the tomato paste darkens, about 2½ minutes. Deglaze the pan with the wine, scraping up the flavorful bits from the bottom. Add the potatoes, carrots, tomatoes, tofu, olives, capers, and vegetable stock. Stir in the bay leaves, cayenne, allspice, and salt. Bring to a boil, turn down the heat, and simmer for 20 minutes.

Add the mushrooms and cook 5 minutes more. Stir in the peas and arrowroot slurry and heat until thickened. Ladle into hot bowls and serve with a slice of Rustic French Bread (page 171).

Time Estimate: Preparation, 20 minutes; cooking, 15 minutes; unsupervised, 20 minutes

Nutritional Profile per Serving: Calories—381; % calories from fat—16%; fat (gm)—7 or 10% daily value; saturated fat (gm)—0; sodium (mg)—635; cholesterol (mg)—0; carbohydrates (gm)—63; dietary fiber (gm)—9; protein (gm)—19. Analysis includes suggested side dishes.

Quinoa MEV with Guacamole Sauce

Serves 4

3 Roma tomatoes
2 bunches spinach

Creole quinoa
1 teaspoon light olive oil with a dash of sesame oil
1 cup finely chopped onion
1/2 cup finely chopped celery
3 cloves garlic, peeled, bashed, and chopped
1 teaspoon dried thyme
1/8 teaspoon ground allspice
1/4 teaspoon ground red pepper (cayenne)
1/4 teaspoon salt
2 bay leaves
1½ cups low-sodium chicken stock (page 207)
1 cup quinoa, well rinsed

Guacamole sauce
1 ripe avocado
1/4 cup yogurt cheese (page 210)
1/8 teaspoon salt
1/4 teaspoon Bali Ethmix (page 218)
1 teaspoon freshly squeezed lime juice
1 tablespoon chopped fresh cilantro

> Try the guacamole with slices of jicama for a delicious, low-fat appetizer.

Slice 2 of the tomatoes and chop the remaining one; set aside. Wash and stem the spinach; steam for 2 minutes, remove from the heat and set aside. Preheat the oven to 350°F (180°C).

To make the Creole quinoa: Heat the oil in a large high-sided skillet over medium high heat and fry the onion until it begins to wilt, 2 minutes. Add the celery and garlic and cook 1 minute more. Sprinkle with the thyme, allspice, cayenne, and salt; add the bay leaves. Pour in the stock and bring to a boil. Add the quinoa, cover, and simmer for 10 to 12 minutes.

Lay a slice of tomato in the bottom of each MEV or other 1-cup mold. Press the water out of the steamed spinach. Save half the spinach to cover the bottoms and divide the rest among the MEV molds on top of the tomato slices. Combine the chopped tomatoes with the Creole quinoa and divide among the 4 molds. Lay the reserved steamed spinach over the top and press down hard. Heat in the preheated oven for 15 to 20 minutes or until warmed through.

To make the sauce: Peel the avocado; discard the skin and pit. Push the flesh through a strainer to render it perfectly smooth. Stir in the yogurt, salt, spice mix, and lime juice. Scatter the cilantro over the top.

To serve: Invert and release each mold onto a flat pan without sides. Slide each mold onto a dinner plate and serve with a Broiled Tomato half (page 161) and a Swift Roasted Butternut Quarter (page 164). Spoon a serving of the guacamole sauce into the bowl of each squash quarter.

Time Estimate: Preparation, 20 minutes; cooking, 15 minutes

Nutritional Profile per Serving: Calories—331; % calories from fat—32%; fat (gm)—12 or 19% daily value; saturated fat (gm)—2; sodium (mg)—185; cholesterol (mg)—0; carbohydrates (gm)—52; dietary fiber (gm)—10; protein (gm)—12. Analysis includes suggested side dishes.

Risi Bisi MEV

Serves 4

2 bags Uncle Ben's Boil-n-Bag Converted Rice or 2 cups cooked rice
12 sun-dried tomato halves
1 medium sweet onion, finely diced
1/2 teaspoon light olive oil with a dash of toasted sesame oil
3 cups frozen petit peas
1 cup chopped arugula leaves
1 tablespoon chopped parsley stalks
1/4 teaspoon salt
1/4 teaspoon freshly ground black pepper
12 large basil leaves
1/2 cup de-alcoholized Chardonnay wine
2 tablespoons freshly grated Parmesan cheese
1/2 teaspoon balsamic vinegar

Cook the boil-n-bag rice uncovered in a 2-quart (2-liter) saucepan in 8 cups of water for 10 minutes.

Preheat the oven to 350°F (180°C).

Soak the sun-dried tomato halves in hot water to cover in a small saucepan for 10 minutes and then chop into 1/2-inch (1.2-cm) slices. Fry the onion in the oil in a high-sided pan over medium high heat for 1 minute. Add the sun-dried tomatoes, and stir until the onions are transparent, about 1 more minute. Add 1 cup of the peas to the onions and tomatoes and cook for 2 minutes. Add the arugula, 1 cup of the rice, the parsley stalks, salt, and pepper and mix thoroughly. Gently tear 6 of the basil leaves into the rice and pea mixture and leave on low heat.

Spray 4 MEV or other 1-cup molds with vegetable oil cooking spray. Using a wet spoon, press 1/4 cup of the remaining rice into the bottom and sides of each mold. Divide the rice and pea mixture among the molds and press down hard with the back of a large spoon or small ladle. Bake in the preheated oven for 20 minutes or until heated through.

To make the sauce: Cook the remaining 2 cups of peas in 2 tablespoons of water in a small saucepan for 3 minutes. Drain off the liquid and pour the peas into a blender. Add the remaining basil leaves, the wine, Parmesan cheese, and balsamic vinegar. Blend on high speed until very smooth.

To serve: Invert each mold onto a plate and release. Pour some of the sauce around each rice mold with a spoonful on top. Garnish with a basil leaf. Arrange Steamed Acorn Squash slices (page 157) and Steamed Broccoli (page 151) around the MEV.

Time Estimate: Preparation, 15 minutes; cooking, 10 minutes

Nutritional Profile per Serving: Calories—341; % calories from fat—8%; fat (gm)—3 or 5% daily value; saturated fat (gm)—0; sodium (mg)—610; cholesterol (mg)—2; carbohydrates (gm)—67; dietary fiber (gm)—14; protein (gm)—16. Analysis includes suggested side dishes.

I recommend Uncle Ben's Converted Rice when long-grain white rice is called for in a recipe. It is milled with a special process that uses steam to push the nutrients from the bran layer into the rice. This white rice is close to brown in nutritional value yet retains the more refined quality of white rice.

Uncle Ben's also offers their converted rice in a Boil-n-Bag form, one of which takes 10 minutes to cook, the other 5 minutes. Both are very acceptable.

Dal MEV with Yogurt Chutney Sauce

Serves 4

2 cups dried red lentils, rinsed and drained
1 teaspoon light olive oil with a dash of toasted sesame oil
1 cup chopped onion
2 cloves garlic, peeled, bashed, and chopped
2 tablespoons India Ethmix (page 218)
1/8 teaspoon salt
1/2 cup chopped dates
1/4 cup shelled pistachio nuts
2 tablespoons Major Grey's mango chutney

Sauce
1/4 cup yogurt cheese (page 210)
3 tablespoons plain yogurt
1 tablespoon Major Grey's mango chutney
1 teaspoon India Ethmix (page 218)

Stir the red lentils into 4 cups of water in a large saucepan and bring to a boil. Turn the heat way down and simmer 15 minutes.

Preheat the oven to 350°F (180°C).

While the lentils are simmering, heat a large high-sided frying pan, add the oil, and fry the onions for about 2 minutes or until they start to wilt. Add the garlic, seasoning mix, and salt and cook to warm the spices, about 2 minutes. Pour the cooked lentils into the pan and stir in the dates, pistachios, and chutney. Spoon into 4 greased MEV or other 1-cup molds and bake in the preheated oven 15 minutes or until heated through.

For the sauce: In a small bowl, combine the sauce ingredients and stir until smooth.

To serve: Unmold each MEV onto a hot plate and spoon a little sauce over the top. I like to serve it with the colorful Mushroom, Pea, and Pimiento Sauté (page 155).

Time Estimate: Preparation, 15 minutes; cooking, 25 minutes; unsupervised, 15 minutes

---

Nutritional Profile per Serving: Calories—369; % calories from fat—15%; fat (gm)—6 or 10% daily value; saturated fat (gm)—0; sodium (mg)—139; cholesterol (mg)—0; carbohydrates (gm)—64; dietary fiber (gm)—13; protein (gm)—19. Analysis includes suggested side dishes.

Italian MEV with Cannellini and Artichokes

Serves 4

1/4 cup de-alcoholized Chardonnay or other dry
    white wine
12 sun-dried tomato halves
1 bunch spinach leaves, washed and stemmed
1/8 teaspoon salt
1/8 teaspoon freshly ground black pepper
1/2 teaspoon light olive oil with a dash of
    toasted sesame oil
1 clove garlic, peeled, bashed, and chopped

4 Roma tomatoes, chopped
3½ cups low-sodium cannellini
    or Great Northern beans, drained and rinsed
1 (14-ounce or 397-gm) can artichoke bottoms,
    drained and thinly sliced
2 tablespoons toasted pine nuts
1⅛ teaspoons Northwest Italy Ethmix
    (page 216), divided
1 cantaloupe, peeled, seeded, and sliced

Bring the wine to a boil in a small saucepan. Drop in the sun-dried tomatoes, remove from the heat, and let steep for 10 minutes. Drain, reserving the liquid, and chop. Set aside.

Spray 4 MEV molds or other 1-cup molds with vegetable oil cooking spray. Lay large spinach leaves in the bottom and up the sides of each mold so that the smoother side of the leaf faces out and the stem end sticks up and over the top of the mold. Dust the spinach with the salt and pepper.

Preheat the oven to 350°F (180°C).

Heat the oil in a large frying pan over medium high heat and add the sun-dried tomatoes, garlic, and 1/2 of the chopped tomatoes, stirring to cook. Add 3 cups of the beans, half the sliced artichoke bottoms, the pine nuts, and 1 teaspoon of the spice mix. Continue to cook 2 minutes or until heated through. Stir until well blended. Spoon equal portions of the bean mixture into each mold and press down with a spoon. Heat the Italian MEV in the preheated oven for 20 minutes.

For the sauce: Whiz the remaining beans, artichoke bottoms, chopped tomatoes, seasoning mix, and reserved liquid from the sun-dried tomatoes in a blender until smooth, about 1 minute. Strain into a saucepan and bring to a boil slowly. If it is too thick, add more wine.

To serve: Pour 2 tablespoons of sauce onto a heated plate and tip a mold upside down onto the puddle of sauce. Serve the cantaloupe slices along either side of the MEV.

Time Estimate: Preparation, 15 minutes; cooking, 23 minutes; unsupervised, 10 minutes

---

Nutritional Profile per Serving: Calories—402; % calories from fat—13%; fat (gm)—6 or 10% daily value; saturated fat (gm)—1; sodium (mg)—324; cholesterol (mg)—0; carbohydrates (gm)—74; dietary fiber (gm)—15; protein (gm)—20. Analysis includes suggested side dishes.

Moroccan Orange Garbanzo MEV

Serves 4

2 medium carrots, peeled and cut into chunks
1/4 teaspoon salt, divided
1/8 teaspoon freshly ground black pepper, divided
1/16 teaspoon grated nutmeg
2 tablespoons rice wine vinegar
1/4 teaspoon ground ginger
1/4 teaspoon mild chili powder
1/2 teaspoon light olive oil with a dash of toasted sesame oil
1 medium onion, finely chopped
3 cups cooked or canned low-sodium garbanzo beans, drained and rinsed
1/3 cup raisins
2 teaspoons Morocco Ethmix (page 218)
2 tablespoons toasted sliced almonds, divided
1 tablespoon sesame tahini
1/4 cup orange juice

Sauce

1 cup orange juice
2 tablespoons raisins
1 tablespoon sesame tahini
1 teaspoon Morocco Ethmix
2 teaspoons arrowroot

Garnish

2 tablespoons raisins
1 tablespoon toasted sliced almonds

Preheat the oven to 350°F (180°C).

Cut the carrots into thin slices, set into a steamer platform and sprinkle with 1/8 teaspoon of the salt, 1/16 teaspoon of the pepper and the nutmeg. Steam over boiling water for 4 minutes or until tender.

While the carrots are steaming, combine the rice wine vinegar, the remaining salt and pepper, ground ginger and chili powder in a medium bowl. Add the steamed carrots, stirring to coat and set aside to marinate.

Heat the oil in a high sided skillet over medium high heat. Fry the onions until they begin to wilt, about 2 minutes. Add the garbanzo beans and raisins, mix well and heat through. Add the Morocco Ethmix and mash with a fork or potato masher. Add the steamed carrots with their marinade and continue mashing. Stir in the almonds and tahini, mashing the ingredients together as you stir. The beans and carrots should be well mashed when you are finished.

Add the orange juice and mix well. Spray the MEV molds or other 1-cup molds with pan spray. Spoon the filling into the molds and press down hard. Place the molds in the preheated oven in a steamer platform and steam over boiling water for 5 minutes to heat through.

For the sauce: Whiz the orange juice, raisins, tahini, seasoning mix, and arrowroot in a blender until the raisins are thoroughly chopped. Heat over medium heat in a small saucepan, stirring constantly, until the sauce thickens and clears.

To serve: Spoon a puddle of sauce on each of 4 hot plates and invert the MEVs on top. Drizzle with the rest of the sauce and garnish with raisins and almonds. Serve with Steamed Kale (page 155) and Couscous with Mint (page 158).

Time Estimate: Preparation, 25 minutes; cooking, 11 minutes

Nutritional Profile per Serving: Calories—1333; % calories from fat—22%; fat (gm)—9 or 13% daily value; saturated fat (gm)—1; sodium (mg)—201; cholesterol (mg)—0; carbohydrates (gm)—59; dietary fiber (gm)—8; protein (gm)—10. Analysis includes suggested side dishes.

Thai MEV with Tofu and Water Chestnuts

Serves 4

Thai mashed potatoes
2 medium russet potatoes, peeled and cut into large chunks
1 small or 1/2 large sweet potato, peeled and cut into large chunks
1/2 cup warm nonfat milk
1/2 teaspoon Thailand Ethmix (page 217)
1/8 teaspoon natural coconut essence

Sauce
1 mango, peeled and sliced into 1/4-inch-thick (.6-cm) slices
1/2 cup de-alcoholized Chardonnay wine
1 tablespoon balsamic vinegar
4 Kaffir lime leaves
1 tablespoon lemon grass, cut in 1/2-inch (1.25-cm) strips
Zest of 1/2 lemon, cut into strips
10 fresh basil leaves

Filling
8 ounces (227 gm) firm 1% tofu, cut into 1/2-inch (1.25-cm) dice
2 teaspoons low-sodium soy sauce
20 cilantro leaves
16 canned water chestnuts, cut into quarters
4 small whole red chilies

Garnish
4 large cilantro leaves
1 ripe papaya, peeled, seeded, and sliced

Cook the white and sweet potatoes together in boiling water for 20 minutes. Drain and place a clean dish towel in the pan on top of the potatoes and allow them to dry out on a warm burner. When they show a mealy surface, press them through a ricer or sieve into a warm bowl. Stir in the warm milk, seasoning mix, and coconut essence. Set the mashed potatoes aside.

Preheat the oven to 350°F (180°C).

For the sauce: Simmer the mango slices, wine, vinegar, lime leaves, lemon grass, lemon zest, and basil in a small covered saucepan over low heat for 10 minutes. Discard the herbs and pour the cooked mangoes and liquid into a blender; process until smooth.

For the filling: Combine the tofu, soy sauce, cilantro, and water chestnuts in a bowl.

To assemble the MEV: Spray 4 MEV or other 1-cup molds with vegetable oil cooking spray and lay a whole chili pepper in the bottom of each one. Pipe some of the mashed potatoes into each mold, covering the bottom and sides. Save a little for the top. Divide the filling among the 4 molds, press down, and cover with the rest of the potatoes. Bake in the preheated oven for 20 minutes or until heated through.

To serve: Spoon a puddle of mango sauce onto each plate and place the MEV on top. Arrange Steamed Bok Choy (page 151) and papaya slices on each side. Garnish each with a cilantro leaf.

Time Estimate: Preparation, 25 minutes; cooking, 30 minutes; unsupervised, 20 minutes

Nutritional Profile per Serving: Calories—341; % calories from fat—4%; fat (gm)—2 or 2% daily value; saturated fat (gm)—0; sodium (mg)—299; cholesterol (mg)—0; carbohydrates (gm)—74; dietary fiber (gm)—9; protein (gm)—13. Analysis includes suggested side dishes.

Cajun MEV with Black-Eyed Peas and Collard Greens

Serves 4

3 large (3 inches or 7.5 cm from top to bottom)
   red bell peppers or 1 16½ oz. (582 gm) jar
   roasted peppers
1 (1/2-pound or 252-gm) bunch collard greens, heavy stalks
   removed (reserve 8 whole leaves)
1/4 teaspoon ground red pepper (cayenne)
1/4 teaspoon ground cumin

1/4 teaspoon salt
1 tablespoon freshly squeezed lemon juice
2 (15.5-ounce or 440-gm) cans
   black-eyed peas, drained and rinsed
3/4 teaspoon chipotle sauce, divided
2 fresh Roma tomatoes, chopped
1/2 teaspoon dried thyme

Cut the bottoms and tops off the peppers. Slice through the peppers top to bottom, remove the seeds, and cut each one in 3 pieces. Lay in the bottom platform of a Stack and Steam or other large steamer over boiling water and steam for 20 minutes. Remove from the heat and seal in a Ziploc bag to continue steaming for at least 10 minutes. The skin should now peel off easily. Set aside 1 whole pepper (you will need 1 cup of steamed pepper strips) for the sauce.

Lay the first bunch of collard leaves in a neat pile, one atop the other. Roll the leaves, lengthwise, into a tight "cigar" and cut crosswise into 1/4–inch-thick (7-cm-thick) slices.

Preheat the oven to 350°F (180°C). Spread the chopped collard greens on a large cutting board and dust with the cayenne, cumin, and salt. Sprinkle the lemon juice over the greens and toss with your hands to mix. Put the shredded greens in the top platform of a Stack and Steam or other large steamer and scatter the black-eyed peas over the top. Lay the whole collard leaves on top of the black-eyed peas and steam for 12 minutes. Remove from the heat, set the whole collard greens aside, and thoroughly mix 1/2 teaspoon of the chipotle sauce into the chopped greens and black-eyed peas.

Spray each of 4 MEV molds or other 1–cup molds with vegetable oil cooking spray and line the bottom and half of one side of each mold with the steamed red pepper pieces. Place a whole collard leaf on the other side of the mold, with the right side of the leaf facing out and overlapping the pepper on the inside. Spoon the black-eyed pea and shredded collard greens mixture into the mold and press down hard. Heat for 20 minutes in a preheated oven.

For the sauce: Whiz the remaining red bell pepper (or 1 cup canned roasted bell pepper from a jar), the tomato, thyme, and remaining 1/4 teaspoon of chipotle sauce for about 1 minute in a blender. Press through a sieve into a small saucepan and heat to simmering.

To serve: Put 2 tablespoons of sauce in a puddle on each plate and set a Cajun MEV on top. Serve Grilled Zucchini (page 159) and Grilled Sweet Potato halves (page 166) on the side.

Time Estimate: Preparation, 20 minutes; cooking, 42 minutes; unsupervised, 20 minutes

Nutritional Profile per Serving: Calories—287; % calories from fat—4%; fat (gm)—1 or 2% daily value; saturated fat (gm)—0; sodium (mg)—492; cholesterol (mg)—0; carbohydrates (gm)—58; dietary fiber (gm)—21; protein (gm)—15. Analysis includes suggested side dishes.

Polish MEV with Apples and Beets

Serves 4

1 bunch collard greens, heavy stems removed
1 (15-ounce or 425-gm) can pickled beet slices
1/2 teaspoon light olive oil with a dash of sesame oil
1 cup finely chopped onion
16 medium mushrooms, sliced across the top
1 tablespoon Poland Ethmix (page 217)
3 cups peeled, chopped tart cooking apple
1/8 teaspoon salt

1/8 teaspoon ground white pepper
4 slices Rye Bread (page 172)

Sauce
1/4 cup pickled beet juice
1 teaspoon balsamic vinegar
15 medium basil leaves
1/2 teaspoon arrowroot

Preheat the oven to 350°F (180°C). Steam the collard leaves for 3 minutes or until wilted but still bright green; remove from the heat and cool. Drain the beets, reserving the liquid for the sauce. Spray 4 MEV molds or other 1-cup molds with vegetable oil cooking spray and line each with the collard leaves. Drop 6 beet slices into each one.

Preheat a large sauté pan over medium high heat and add the oil. Fry the onions until they just start to brown, about 2 minutes, then add the mushrooms. Stir in the seasoning mix and cook 2 minutes more. Add the chopped apple, salt, and white pepper and continue cooking 2 more minutes. Remove from the heat and spoon equal portions into each lined mold. Top each with a slice of rye bread, cut to fit, and press down hard. Place in the preheated oven and heat through, about 20 minutes.

For the sauce: Whiz the sauce ingredients together in a blender until smooth. Pour into a small saucepan and heat just until it thickens.

To serve: Arrange a Baked Russet Potato half (page 166), a fennel half (page 154) and a serving of Swiss Chard (page 158) on each of 4 hot plates. Unmold a Polish MEV onto each plate and spoon sauce over it.

Time Estimate: Preparation, 25 minutes; cooking, 11 minutes; unsupervised, 20 minutes

Nutritional Profile per Serving: Calories—307; % calories from fat—6%; fat (gm)—2 or 3% daily value; saturated fat (gm)—0; sodium (mg)—697; cholesterol (mg)—0; carbohydrates (gm)—72; dietary fiber (gm)—14; protein (gm)—8. Analysis includes suggested side dishes.

Mexican MEV with Beans, Peppers, and Jicama

Serves 4

1 tablespoon light olive oil with a dash of toasted sesame oil
1 large onion, sliced
2 cloves garlic, peeled, bashed, and sliced
1 teaspoon summer savory
1½ teaspoons chipotle sauce, divided
2 cups dried white beans, soaked overnight or quick-soaked (page 22) and drained
2 cups boiling water
1 tablespoon finely sliced cilantro leaves plus 13 large whole cilantro leaves
1/4 teaspoon salt, divided
1/4 heaping cup diced jicama
2 large red bell peppers, roasted and cut into strips, 3 tablespoons reserved for sauce
2 medium tomatoes, coarsely chopped

To cook the beans: Heat the oil in a pressure cooker and fry the onion, garlic, savory, and 1/4 teaspoon of the chipotle sauce over high heat, stirring often so as not to scorch them, for 2 minutes. Stir in the soaked beans and pour the boiling water over all. Attach the lid and bring up to full pressure. When the pressure is up, reduce the heat to low and cook for 9 minutes. Remove from the heat and release the steam immediately under cold running water.

Preheat the oven to 350°F (180°C).

Pour the beans through a strainer, reserving the liquid in a large bowl. Put 2 cups of cooked beans into a bowl and mash roughly with a fork. Stir in 1 teaspoon of the chipotle sauce, the sliced cilantro leaves, and 1/8 teaspoon of the salt. Add the diced jicama and 2 cups of whole beans to the seasoned mashed beans in the bowl and mix well.

Spray 4 MEV molds or other 1-cup molds with vegetable oil cooking spray. Lay 1 large cilantro leaf in the bottom of each mold and arrange the roasted red bell pepper strips over the bottom and up the sides. Fill each mold with the beans and jicama mixture and press down. Bake in the preheated oven 20 minutes or until heated through.

For the sauce: Whiz the tomatoes, reserved roasted peppers, remaining beans, 1/2 cup of the bean juice, whole cilantro leaves, the remaining 1/4 teaspoon chipotle sauce, and the remaining 1/8 teaspoon salt in a blender for a minute or two or until very smooth. Press the sauce through a sieve into a bowl before serving.

To serve: Unmold each Mexican MEV onto a hot plate. Pour a band of sauce around it and add a slice of hot prepared polenta (generally available in the specialty food section of the supermarket) and a serving of Steamed Collard Greens (page 153) to complete the plate.

Time Estimate: Preparation, 20 minutes; cooking, 25 minutes; unsupervised, 55 minutes

Nutritional Profile per Serving: Calories—494; % calories from fat—6%; fat (gm)—4 or 5% daily value; saturated fat (gm)—0; sodium (mg)—353; cholesterol (mg)—0; carbohydrates (gm)—94; dietary fiber (gm)—27; protein (gm)—27. Analysis includes suggested side dishes.

ROASTING OR STEAMING PEPPERS

To roast peppers, cut the top and bottom off each pepper, cut the remaining cylinder in half lengthwise, and discard the seeds, pith, and stem. Cut each pepper in half again. Lay the 4 pieces and the top and bottom on a broiler pan. Broil 2 or 3 inches (5 to 7.5 cm) from the heating element for 10 minutes or until the skin is black and blistered. Transfer to a paper bag, close tightly, and allow to cool for 20 minutes. Peel off the skin and use at once, or place in a resealable plastic bag, press out the air, date, and freeze for up to 6 months.

Steamed peppers not only peel easily but have the added benefit of keeping a bright red color. Cut the tops off the peppers to be steamed, remove the seeds and pith, and steam in a large steamer for 20 minutes.

New England Bean and Brown Bread MEV

Canned brown bread is a new product for me even though it's been around a long time. You will find it in the grocery store next to the baked beans. It's a wonderful bread flavored with molasses and textured with raisins—a perfect complement to New England baked beans. Ask your grocer if you don't find it.

Serves 4

1 teaspoon light olive oil with a dash of toasted sesame oil, divided
1 large white onion, chopped (2 cups)
2 cloves garlic, peeled, bashed, and chopped
1/2 cup fruit-sweetened tomato ketchup
1/2 teaspoon dried summer savory
1/2 teaspoon ground cumin
1/2 teaspoon dry mustard
2 tablespoons balsamic vinegar
3 tablespoons maple syrup
1 cup unsweetened apple cider
3 cups cooked white beans
4 large mushrooms, trimmed and sliced
1/2 teaspoon freshly squeezed lemon juice
1/8 teaspoon salt
1/8 teaspoon freshly ground black pepper
8 thin slices canned brown bread (1/2 can)
1/2 teaspoon arrowroot mixed with 2 tablespoons de-alcoholized red wine (slurry)

Preheat the convection oven to 300°F (150°C) or a conventional oven to 350°F (180°C).

Heat a pressure cooker over high heat and add 1/2 teaspoon of the oil, the onions, and garlic, stirring to cook until translucent, about 3 minutes. Reduce the heat to low and add the ketchup, summer savory, cumin, mustard, and balsamic vinegar; mix together. Stir in the maple syrup, apple cider, and beans. Cover, securing the lid, and bring the pressure up over high heat. Reduce the heat just enough to keep the pressure constant and pressure–cook for 6 minutes. Release the pressure quickly by running cold water over the top. Drain the beans, reserving the liquid. If you don't have a pressure cooker, prepare the above ingredients in a Dutch oven and simmer 30 minutes. Pour cooking liquid into measuring cup.

Heat the remaining 1/2 teaspoon of oil in a frying pan and toss in the mushroom slices, lemon juice, salt, and pepper; fry for 2 minutes or until the mushrooms just begin to wilt. Spray 4 MEV molds or other 1-cup molds with vegetable oil cooking spray and lay a slice of the bread in the bottom of each mold. Drop the mushroom slices on top of the bread. Fill each mold with beans and top with another slice of bread, pressing down hard. Place the molds in the preheated oven for 15 minutes or until heated through.

For the sauce: Pour 1 cup of the reserved bean liquid into the frying pan and stir in the slurry. Heat on medium high to thicken.

To serve: Invert and unmold each MEV on a plate and spoon the sauce over it. Serve with Baked Russet Potato Halves (page 166), Steamed Broccoli (page 151), and Carrots in Tonic Water (page 152) alongside.

Time Estimate: Preparation, 20 minutes; cooking, 13 minutes; unsupervised, 15 minutes

Nutritional Profile per Serving: Calories—587; % calories from fat—8%; fat (gm)—5 or 8% daily value; saturated fat (gm)—0; sodium (mg)—434; cholesterol (mg)—0; carbohydrates (gm)—123; dietary fiber (gm)—18; protein (gm)—22. Analysis includes suggested side dishes.

Shanghai Stuffed Peppers

Serves 4

3 red bell peppers
2 green bell peppers
1 bunch green onions, washed and trimmed
1/2 teaspoon light olive oil with a dash of toasted sesame oil
1/4 teaspoon Shanghai Coastline Ethmix (page 215)
2 cloves garlic, peeled, bashed, and chopped
12 dime-sized slices fresh ginger, finely chopped
1 cup fresh or frozen corn kernels
1 cup frozen peas
2 cups Boiled Rice (page 163)
1/4 teaspoon toasted sesame oil
1 cup de-alcoholized Chardonnay wine
3 tablespoons low-sodium tamari
1 tablespoon cornstarch

shanghaied stuffed peppers

Bring water to a boil in a large steamer. Cut 2 of the red peppers and the 2 green peppers in half lengthwise and trim off the stems, removing the seeds and veins. Cut the top and bottom off the third red pepper. Discard the core and seeds and cut the middle part into long, slender strips to use in the suggested salad. Chop the top and bottom and set aside to add later on in the recipe. Steam the pepper halves and strips in the steamer for 4 minutes. Remove the peppers and set aside to cool.

Finely chop the white bulbs of the green onions. Cut the green part into 1/4-inch (.75-cm) slices and set aside for later. Heat a high-sided pan over medium high heat and add the oil, seasoning mix, garlic, ginger, and chopped onion bulbs and stir-fry for 1 minute. Add the sliced onion tops, corn, reserved chopped red pepper, and peas and stir to mix. Add the rice and stir with the vegetables until heated through. Toss with the toasted sesame oil.

Combine the wine, tamari, and cornstarch in a measuring cup. Pour into the rice mix, stirring to cook the cornstarch and thicken the sauce. When heated through, fill each pepper half with 1 cup of the rice and vegetable mixture.

To serve: Lay a nest of Asian Sunflower Sprout and Red Pepper Salad (page 24) on a plate and arrange a stuffed red bell pepper half next to a stuffed green bell pepper end to end.

Time Estimate: Preparation, 20 minutes; cooking, 10 minutes

Nutritional Profile per Serving: Calories—362; % calories from fat—5%; fat (gm)—2 or 3% daily value; saturated fat (gm)—0; sodium (mg)—740; cholesterol (mg)—0; carbohydrates (gm)—74; dietary fiber (gm)—8; protein (gm)—16. Analysis includes suggested side dishes.

Scandinavian Rutabaga and Wild Mushroom MEV

Serves 4

1 large head dark green Savoy cabbage
1 pound (450 gm) rutabagas, peeled and cut in halves
4 medium new potatoes, peeled and cut in halves
1/2 teaspoon light olive oil with a dash of toasted sesame oil
1½ cups thinly sliced onion
12 fresh mushrooms (preferably wild), thickly sliced
1/4 teaspoon salt
1/8 teaspoon freshly ground black pepper
1 teaspoon Scandinavia Ethmix (page 215)
1 tablespoon balsamic vinegar

Sauce
1/4 cup yogurt cheese (page 210)
2 teaspoons horseradish
2 tablespoons nonfat plain yogurt
1 heaping teaspoon chopped fresh chives

Preheat the oven to 350°F (180°C).

Remove 4 large whole leaves from the outside of the cabbage. Place the leaves in a steamer platform over boiling water and steam for 1 to 2 minutes or until limp enough to line 4 MEV molds or other 1-cup molds. Slice the rest of the cabbage thinly. You should have 3 to 4 cups.

Cook the rutabagas and potatoes in boiling water until just tender, about 18 minutes. Drain and allow to cool.

Heat a high-sided skillet over medium high heat, add the oil, onions, and mushrooms, and fry for 1 minute. Add the sliced cabbage, salt, pepper, and seasoning mix. Cook for 3 minutes or until the cabbage starts to soften. Toss with the balsamic vinegar. Cover the pan and leave it on the burner with the heat turned off while you prepare the cooked vegetables. Cut the rutabagas and potatoes into 1/2-inch (1.25-cm) slices.

Line the molds with the steamed cabbage leaves and layer in the rutabaga slices, cabbage/mushroom mixture, and more rutabaga slices, finishing with potato slices. Push down hard. Bake for 15 to 20 minutes or until heated through.

While the MEVs are heating, stir the sauce ingredients together.

To serve: Unmold each MEV onto a hot plate surrounded by Grated Parsnips and Carrots (page 156) and Steamed Green Beans (page 150). Spoon a little of the horseradish yogurt sauce on the side.

Time Estimate: Preparation, 15 minutes; cooking, 24 minutes; unsupervised, 20 minutes

Nutritional Profile per Serving: Calories—405; % calories from fat—5%; fat (gm)—2 or 3% daily value; saturated fat (gm)—0; sodium (mg)—423; cholesterol (mg)—1; carbohydrates (gm)—89; dietary fiber (gm)—20; protein (gm)—14. Analysis includes suggested side dishes.

Vegetable and Starch Side Dishes

Embracing Vegetables

The greatest, most beneficial change you can make in your approach to a healthier lifestyle is to stop smoking. The second, in my opinion, is to embrace the vegetable!

Mothers everywhere have cried out, "Eat your vegetables!" The U.S. Government has supported the Five-a-Day program that recommends five half-cup servings of fruits and vegetables. The Canadians shoot for Nine-a-Day.

No matter who is saying it or how much, there is truth behind the need for more—a lot more—fresh vegetables in our diets. So what's holding us back?

Here are a few simple ideas and some suggested solutions:

Eat up your vegetables!

- **Maternal backlash:** You can call it rebellion against what you were told was "good for you." It's called growing up— being our own person. Eventually, even if we didn't change, we find ourselves exhorting our own children to "Eat your vegetables!"
  - **Solution:** Make a stand. A new tradition can begin with you! Remember that children learn by watching what you do.
- **Vegicide:** We murder our vegetables. We boil them to death, rob them of color, nutrients, and flavor. No wonder we shun these corpses!
  - **Solution:** Learn how *and* how long to cook vegetables to retain their flavor, color, texture, and nutrients. In the extensive section on vegetables that follows (and throughout this book) we've shown you fresh and creative ways to use dozens of different vegetables.
- **Seasoning:** It's not enough to add salt to the water.
  - **Solution:** Experiment with chopped fresh herb garnishes, with scatterings of dried herbs like dill weed, or with any of my Ethmixes that you can also assemble yourself. See pages 215–219.

• **Buying Fresh and Best in Season:** Some vegetables and many fruits are relatively tasteless because they are picked green and transported to you over long distances out of season.

• **Solution:** Ask your grocer what is Fresh and Best in Season (F.A.B.I.S) and select, whenever possible, what is grown locally. Be sure to always include dark green leafy vegetables (kale, chard, spinach, and collards) and orange roots (sweet potatoes, carrots, various winter squash), and then you'll get the most active nutrition density for your dollar.

The more we shrink the size of the meat serving, the more we will come to rely upon vegetables. The better we prepare these wonderful plants, the greater will be our enjoyment. The more we enjoy change, the longer it will last, and this is the kind of change that will really make an enormous difference in our sense of well-being.

Steamed Asparagus

Serves 4

20 asparagus spears
1/16 teaspoon salt
1/16 teaspoon freshly ground black pepper
1/4 teaspoon dried basil

Bring water to a boil in a large steamer. Lay a doubled piece of waxed paper over one side of the platform. Place the heads of the asparagus spears over the waxed paper and the stems over the open platform and lightly dust with the salt, pepper, and basil. Cover and steam for 3 minutes or until tender but still slightly crisp.

Nutritional Profile per Serving: Calories—17; % calories from fat—8%; fat (gm)—less than 1 or 1% daily value; saturated fat (gm)—0; sodium (mg)—35; cholesterol (mg)—0; carbohydrates (gm)—3; dietary fiber (gm)—2; protein (gm)—3

Steamed Green Beans

Serves 4

1 pound (454 gm) fresh green beans
1/16 teaspoon salt
1/16 teaspoon freshly ground black pepper
1/4 teaspoon Southern France Ethmix (page 216)

Remove the tips, tails, and any strings from the green beans and cut the beans into thirds. Place on a steamer platform and scatter the salt, pepper, and seasoning mix over the top. Toss to mix. Steam over boiling water for 7 minutes. Serve immediately while they still have a crisp-tender texture.

Nutritional Profile per Serving: Calories—35; % calories from fat—13%; fat (gm)—less than 1 or 1% daily value; saturated fat (gm)—0; sodium (mg)—40; cholesterol (mg)—0; carbohydrates (gm)—8; dietary fiber (gm)—4; protein (gm)—2

Steamed Bok Choy

Serves 4

    4 baby bok choy, or 1 large
    1/8 teaspoon salt
    1/16 teaspoon white pepper
    1 tablespoon freshly squeezed lemon juice

Bring water to a boil in a Stack and Steam or other large steamer. Steam the baby bok choy on a platform of the steamer over high heat for 2 minutes. Dust with the salt and white pepper and steam for another 2 minutes.

If you can't get baby bok choy, use a large stalk. Cut it in half lengthwise, then in half crosswise, separating the stem from the leaves. Steam the stem half for 2 minutes, then add the leaves and steam for 2 more minutes. Sprinkle with the lemon juice before serving.

Nutritional Profile per Serving: Calories—13; % calories from fat—12%; fat (gm)—less than 1 or 1% daily value; saturated fat (gm)—0; sodium (mg)—104; cholesterol (mg)—0; carbohydrates (gm)—2; dietary fiber (gm)—2; protein (gm)—2

Steamed Broccoli

Serves 4

    4 cups broccoli florets
    1 tablespoon lemon juice
    1/8 teaspoon salt
    1/16 teaspoon freshly ground black pepper
    1/4 teaspoon dried tarragon

Bring water to a boil in a Stack and Steam or other large steamer. Place the broccoli florets on a steaming platform and steam over medium high heat for 5 to 7 minutes. Remove and sprinkle the broccoli with lemon juice, salt, black pepper, and tarragon.

Nutritional Profile per Serving: Calories—26; % calories from fat—11%; fat (gm)—0 or 1% daily value; saturated fat (gm)—0; sodium (mg)—91; cholesterol (mg)—5; carbohydrates (gm)—5; dietary fiber (gm)—2; protein (gm)—3

Steamed Baby Carrots

Serves 4

    1 pound (454 gm) baby carrots
    1/16 teaspoon salt
    1/16 teaspoon freshly ground white pepper
    1/2 teaspoon dried dill weed

Lay the carrots on a steamer platform of a large steamer. Cover and steam over boiling water for 8 minutes. Remove from the heat, dust with salt and pepper, and scatter dill over the top.

Nutritional Profile per Serving: Calories—43; % calories from fat—13%; fat (gm)—less than 1 or 1% daily value; saturated fat (gm)—0; sodium (mg)—73; cholesterol (mg)—0; carbohydrates (gm)—9; dietary fiber (gm)—4; protein (gm)—0

Carrots in Tonic Water

Serves 4

    4 large carrots, peeled and cut diagonally (2 cups)
    1 cup tonic water
    1/8 teaspoon salt
    1/8 teaspoon white pepper
    1/16 teaspoon grated nutmeg
    1/2 teaspoon arrowroot mixed with 1 teaspoon tonic water (slurry)
    1 teaspoon chopped fresh parsley

Place the carrot slices in a medium saucepan and pour the tonic water over the top. Add the salt and white pepper and cover with a lid. Bring to a boil over high heat; cook for about 5 minutes, then reduce the heat and simmer for 20 minutes. Add nutmeg and parsley to the carrots and pour in the arrowroot slurry, tossing to coat the carrots with a glossy sauce.

Nutritional Profile per Serving: Calories—54; % calories from fat—2%; fat (gm)—less than 1 or 1% daily value; saturated fat (gm)—0; sodium (mg)—94; cholesterol (mg)—0; carbohydrates (gm)—13; dietary fiber (gm)—2; protein (gm)—0

Steamed Caulifower

Serves 4

 1 large head of cauliflower
 1/4 teaspoon Germany Ethmix (page 217)
 1 tablespoon finely chopped fresh parsley

Separate the cauliflower into florets and discard the core. Place the florets in a large steamer over boiling water. Steam for 7 to 11 minutes, depending on the size of the florets. Combine the seasoning mix with the parsley and sprinkle on the cooked cauliflower.

Nutritional Profile per Serving: Calories—11; % calories from fat—8%; fat (gm)—less than 1 or 1% daily value; saturated fat (gm)—0; sodium (mg)—14; cholesterol (mg)—0; carbohydrates (gm)—2; dietary fiber (gm)—0; protein (gm)—0

Steamed Collard Greens

Serves 4

 1 pound (454 gm) collard greens, washed and stemmed
 1/4 teaspoon dried basil
 1 tablespoon freshly squeezed lemon juice

In a large layered steamer, bring water to a boil. Place the collard greens on a platform and sprinkle with basil. Cook over gently boiling water for 8 minutes. Sprinkle lemon juice over the collards just before serving.

Nutritional Profile per Serving: Calories—36; % calories from fat—6%; fat (gm)—less than 1 or 1% daily value; saturated fat (gm)—0; sodium (mg)—23; cholesterol (mg)—0; carbohydrates (gm)—8; dietary fiber (gm)—4; protein (gm)—2

Steamed Fennel Bulbs

Serves 4

2 large fennel bulbs
1/4 teaspoon ground allspice
1/4 teaspoon dried basil

Bring water to a boil in a Stack and Steam or other large steamer. Trim the stalks and stringy parts off the fennel bulbs. Cut the bulbs in half lengthwise, place on a steamer platform, and sprinkle with allspice and basil. Steam for 10 minutes.

Nutritional Profile per Serving: Calories—37; % calories from fat—6%; fat (gm)—less than 1 or 1% daily value; saturated fat (gm)—0; sodium (mg)—61; cholesterol (mg)—0; carbohydrates (gm)—9; dietary fiber (gm)—5; protein (gm)—2

Steamed Mixed Greens

Serves 4

1 bunch mustard greens, washed, stemmed, and chopped
1 bunch collard greens, washed, stemmed, and chopped
1 bunch Swiss chard, washed, stemmed, and chopped
1/8 teaspoon salt
1/8 teaspoon freshly ground black pepper
1/8 teaspoon grated nutmeg

Bring water to a boil in a large steamer. Spread the chopped greens on the cutting board. Sprinkle with salt, pepper, and nutmeg and toss to mix. Combine the chopped greens on a platform of the steamer and steam for 4 to 6 minutes.

Nutritional Profile per Serving: Calories—42; % calories from fat—8%; fat (gm)—less than 1 or 1% daily value; saturated fat (gm)—0; sodium (mg)—198; cholesterol (mg)—0; carbohydrates (gm)—9; dietary fiber (gm)—4; protein (gm)—3

Steamed Kale

Serves 4

12 ounces (340 gm) kale, washed, with heavy stems removed
1 teaspoon dried dill
1/8 teaspoon salt

Bring 2 cups of water to a boil in a large steamer. Place the kale on a platform in the steamer, cover, and steam for 4 minutes over medium high heat. Remove the platform, set it on a plate and sprinkle kale with the dill and salt. Toss to mix.

Nutritional Profile per Serving: Calories—29; % calories from fat—11%; fat (gm)—less than 1 or 1% daily value; saturated fat (gm)—0; sodium (mg)—88; cholesterol (mg)—0; carbohydrates (gm)—5; dietary fiber (gm)—2; protein (gm)—2

Mushroom, Pea, and Pimiento Sauté

Serves 4

12 medium mushrooms, cut into quarters
2 tablespoons freshly squeezed lemon juice
2 cups frozen peas, defrosted
1/4 cup chopped pimientos
1/8 teaspoon salt
1/8 teaspoon freshly ground black pepper

Toss the mushrooms with the lemon juice and fry them in a hot frying pan over high heat for 2 to 3 minutes or until they start to brown. Add the peas and pimientos and cook just long enough for the peas to heat through. Sprinkle salt and pepper over the vegetables and serve immediately.

Nutritional Profile per Serving: Calories—77; % calories from fat—7%; fat (gm)—less than 1 or 1% daily value; saturated fat (gm)—0; sodium (mg)—74; cholesterol (mg)—0; carbohydrates (gm)—14; dietary fiber (gm)—5; protein (gm)—5

Lemon-Fried Shiitakes

Serves 4

Juice of 1/2 lemon
12 large shiitake mushrooms, stems cut off
1/16 teaspoon salt
1/16 teaspoon freshly ground black pepper

Pour the lemon juice into a heated sauteé pan and drop in the shiitakes, dark side down, in a single layer. Dust lightly with salt and pepper. Cook for 2 minutes, turn, and remove from the heat, allowing the mushrooms to finish cooking in the retained heat.

Nutritional Profile per Serving: Calories—32; % calories from fat—4%; fat (gm)—less than 1 or 1% daily value; saturated fat (gm)—0; sodium (mg)—36; cholesterol (mg)—0; carbohydrates (gm)—8; dietary fiber (gm)—1; protein (gm)—0

Grated Parsnips and Carrots

Serves 4

4 medium parsnips, peeled
4 medium carrots, peeled
1/4 cup raisins
2 teaspoons Southern France Ethmix (page 216)
1/4 teaspoon salt

Cut the carrots and parsnips into 4-inch (10-cm) lengths to fit the feeder of your food processor. Grate on the larger-hole grating disk or by hand. Steam the grated parsnips and carrots with the raisins, seasoning mix, and salt on the platform of a large steamer over boiling water for 7 minutes.

Nutritional Profile per Serving: Calories—168; % calories from fat—3%; fat (gm)—less than 1 or 1% daily value; saturated fat (gm)—0; sodium (mg)—174; cholesterol (mg)—0; carbohydrates (gm)—41; dietary fiber (gm)—9; protein (gm)—3

Steamed Spinach

Serves 4

    2 bunches fresh spinach, washed and stemmed
    1/16 teaspoon salt
    1/16 teaspoon freshly ground black pepper

Spread the washed spinach on the kitchen work surface and sprinkle with the salt and pepper. Steam in a large steamer for 2 minutes or until just wilted.

Nutritional Profile per Serving: Calories—18; % calories from fat—14%; fat (gm)—less than 1 or 1% daily value; saturated fat (gm)—0; sodium (mg)—98; cholesterol (mg)—0; carbohydrates (gm)—3; dietary fiber (gm)—2; protein (gm)—2

Steamed Acorn Squash

Serves 4

    2 acorn squash, cut in half with seeds removed
    1/8 teaspoon salt
    1/16 teaspoon freshly ground white pepper
    1/4 teaspoon dried tarragon

Bring water to a boil in a large steamer. Cut the squash halves into 1-inch (2.5-cm) slices and place them on the steaming platform. Sprinkle with salt, white pepper, and tarragon and steam, covered, over medium high heat for 10 to 12 minutes, or until tender.

Nutritional Profile per Serving: Calories—48; % calories from fat—2%; fat (gm)—less than 1 or 1% daily value; saturated fat (gm)—0; sodium (mg)—71; cholesterol (mg)—0; carbohydrates (gm)—12; dietary fiber (gm)—4; protein (gm)—0

Swiss Chard

Serves 4

1 pound (454 gm) Swiss chard, stems trimmed and discarded
1/4 teaspoon ground allspice
1/4 teaspoon dried basil

Bring water to a boil in a large steamer. Lay the Swiss chard leaves on the steamer platform and sprinkle with allspice and basil. Steam for 6 to 8 minutes, or until tender.

Nutritional Profile per Serving: Calories—22; % calories from fat—10%; fat (gm)—less than 1 or 1% daily value; saturated fat (gm)—0; sodium (mg)—241; cholesterol (mg)—0; carbohydrates (gm)—4; dietary fiber (gm)—2; protein (gm)—2

Couscous with Mint

Serves 4

1 bay leaf
1/4 teaspoon Shanghai Coastline Ethmix (page 215)
2 fresh whole mint leaves
1 cup instant couscous

Garnish
1/16 teaspoon Shanghai Coastline Ethmix
4 large mint leaves, cut in thin strips (chiffonade)

Bring 2 cups of water to a boil over high heat in a medium saucepan with the bay leaf, seasoning mix, and mint leaves. Remove from the heat and pour in the couscous while gently shaking the pan. Cover and let set, off the heat, for at least 5 minutes or until you are ready to serve it.

To serve: Remove the bay leaf and mint leaves and scoop a portion of the couscous onto each plate. Garnish the couscous with a dusting of seasoning mix and the fine strips of mint.

Nutritional Profile per Serving: Calories—50; % calories from fat—9%; fat (gm)—less than 1 or 1% daily value; saturated fat (gm)—0; sodium (mg)—2; cholesterol (mg)—0; carbohydrates (gm)—10; dietary fiber (gm)—0; protein (gm)—2

Grilled Zucchini

Serves 4

2 small green zucchini, cut in half lengthwise
2 small yellow summer squash, cut in half lengthwise
1/16 teaspoon ground rosemary
1/16 teaspoon salt
1/16 teaspoon freshly ground black pepper

Dust the squash with rosemary, salt, and pepper and place cut side down on a heated grill for 5 minutes. Turn on the skin side and grill for 5 more minutes. Alternatively, you can broil the squash in the oven for 3 to 5 minutes per side.

Nutritional Profile per Serving: Calories—4; % calories from fat—17%; fat (gm)—less than 1 or 1% daily value; saturated fat (gm)—0; sodium (mg)—33; cholesterol (mg)—0; carbohydrates (gm)—0; dietary fiber (gm)—0; protein (gm)—0

Beet and Potato Purée

Serves 4

3 medium beets, stems and root ends removed, cut in half
2 medium russet potatoes, cut into quarters
1 teaspoon Poland Ethmix (page 217)
1/4 teaspoon freshly ground black pepper
1/4 teaspoon salt

Cook the beets and potatoes with 1 cup of water in a pressure cooker for 15 minutes on high pressure (30 minutes in a conventional covered saucepan). Release the pressure by running cold water over the top of the pressure cooker. Remove the lid and peel the beets and potatoes as soon as they are cool enough to handle. Mash with a potato masher just to break up the big pieces, then beat with a hand mixer. The potato should be pretty well mashed with discernible, but small, chunks of beets showing. Scatter the seasoning mix, pepper, and salt over the top and stir in with the mixer. Reheat in the microwave or in a double boiler and serve.

Nutritional Profile per Serving: Calories—79; % calories from fat—6%; fat (gm)—less than 1 or 1% daily value; saturated fat (gm)—0; sodium (mg)—167; cholesterol (mg)—0; carbohydrates (gm)—18; dietary fiber (gm)—2; protein (gm)—2

Indian Bulgur Pilaf

Serves 4

1/2 teaspoon light olive oil with a dash of toasted sesame oil
1/2 cup chopped onion
1½ teaspoons India Ethmix (page 218)
1/4 cup currants
1/2 cup bulgur wheat
2 cups low-sodium chicken stock (page 207) or vegetable stock (page 210)
1/4 cup roughly chopped pistachio nuts

Heat the oil in a large saucepan. Add the onions and fry until they start to wilt, about 2 minutes. Stir frequently so they don't brown. Add the seasoning mix, currants, and bulgur, stirring to coat the wheat with the seasoning and heat it through. Pour in the stock, bring to a boil, then turn down to the lowest heat and simmer 15 minutes. Stir in the pistachio nuts and serve.

Nutritional Profile per Serving: Calories—293; % calories from fat—19%; fat (gm)—6 or 9% daily value; saturated fat (gm)—1; sodium (mg)—103; cholesterol (mg)—0 carbohydrates (gm)—54; dietary fiber (gm)—12; protein (gm)—10

Roasted Corn with Tamari and Lime Juice

Serves 4

4 ears fresh corn, husks removed
1/4 cup freshly squeezed lime juice
1 teaspoon low-sodium tamari
1/4 teaspoon ground red pepper (cayenne)

Preheat the grill or oven to its highest heat. Combine the lime juice, tamari, and cayenne and brush the corn with the mixture. Place the corn on the grill and cook for 15 minutes, brushing with the sauce and turning every 5 minutes. Save a little to brush on at the very end just before you serve them. You won't need butter with this recipe!

Nutritional Profile per Serving: Calories—137; % calories from fat—11%; fat (gm)—2 or 3% daily value; saturated fat (gm)—0; sodium (mg)—74; cholesterol (mg)—0; carbohydrates (gm)—32; dietary fiber (gm)—4; protein (gm)—4

Wine-Simmered Butter Beans

Serves 4

1/2 teaspoon light olive oil with a dash of toasted sesame oil
1/2 cup chopped onion
2 cloves garlic, bashed, peeled, and chopped
1/2 teaspoon Southern France Ethmix (page 216)
1/8 teaspoon freshly ground black pepper
1/4 cup de-alcoholized Chardonnay
2 (15-ounce or 425-gm) cans butter beans, drained and rinsed
1/4 teaspoon arrowroot mixed with 1 tablespoon de-alcoholized Chardonnay (slurry)

Heat the oil in a high-sided skillet over medium high heat and fry the onions until they start to wilt, 2 minutes. Add the garlic, seasoning mix, and pepper and cook for another minute. Pour in the wine, stirring to mix, and add the beans. Cover and simmer very gently for 5 minutes. Set the lid aside, remove from the heat, and stir in the slurry. Return to the heat to thicken (which will happen almost immediately), then serve.

Nutritional Profile per Serving: Calories—129; % calories from fat—7%; fat (gm)—1 or 2% daily value; saturated fat (gm)—0; sodium (mg)—226; cholesterol (mg)—0; carbohydrates (gm)—23; dietary fiber (gm)—7; protein (gm)—8

Broiled Tomatoes

Serves 4

2 large tomatoes, cut in half crosswise
1/16 teaspoon salt
1/16 teaspoon white pepper

Set the 4 tomato halves, cut side up, on a broiler pan, spray lightly with olive oil cooking spray, and dust with salt and pepper. Broil without turning for 8 minutes.

Nutritional Profile per Serving: Calories—19; % calories from fat—14%; fat (gm)—less than 1 or 1% daily value; saturated fat (gm)—0; sodium (mg)—75; cholesterol (mg)—0; carbohydrates (gm)—4; dietary fiber (gm)—0; protein (gm)—0

Potato Halves with Parmesan Yogurt Sauce

Serves 4

2 potatoes, scrubbed and cut in half crosswise
4 tablespoons yogurt cheese (page 210)
1 tablespoon freshly grated Parmesan cheese
2 teaspoons chopped fresh chives
1/8 teaspoon white pepper

Preheat the oven to 400°F (200°C). Cut a cross 3/4 inch (2 cm) down on the skin end of each potato half. Arrange the potato halves in a microwavable glass dish with a lid. Microwave, covered, on high power for 10 minutes. Remove the potatoes from the microwave, set each half cut side down on the dish, and bake, uncovered, in a preheated convection oven for 10 minutes or in a conventional oven for 15.

In a small mixing bowl, stir together the yogurt cheese, the freshly grated Parmesan cheese, chopped chives, and white pepper. Spoon onto the opened potatoes.

Nutritional Profile per Serving: Calories—191; % calories from fat—5%; fat (gm)—less than 1 or 2% daily value; saturated fat (gm)—0; sodium (mg)—64; cholesterol (mg)—1; carbohydrates (gm)—41; dietary fiber (gm)—4; protein (gm)—6

Steamed Tiny Red Potatoes

Serves 4

1 generous pound tiny red potatoes
1/16 teaspoon salt
1/16 teaspoon freshly ground black pepper
1/2 teaspoon dried dill weed

Steam the potatoes on the platform of a large steamer over boiling water for 15 minutes. Remove the platform and sprinkle salt, pepper, and dill over the top.

Nutritional Profile per Serving: Calories—119; % calories from fat—4%; fat (gm)—less than 1 or 1% daily value; saturated fat (gm)—0; sodium (mg)—42; cholesterol (mg)—0; carbohydrates (gm)—27; dietary fiber (gm)—3; protein (gm)—3

Boiled Rice

For more years than I care to remember, this has been my method of cooking long-grain white rice. It comes from an early Indonesian technique in which the rice was wrapped in a cone of large green leaves and steamed over water. It works perfectly every time.

Makes 3 cups or 4 (3/4-cup) servings

    1/4 teaspoon salt
    1 cup converted long-grain white rice

Bring 6 cups of water to a boil in a medium saucepan. Add the salt and rice and bring back to a boil partially covered. Remove the cover and maintain the boil for 10 minutes. Pour the rice and water through a strainer. Put fresh water into the saucepan and bring to a boil over high heat. Set the strainer of rice on top of the saucepan and cover. Reduce the heat to medium and steam for 10 minutes. Turn the heat to the lowest possible setting until ready to serve.

Nutritional Profile per Serving: Calories—169; % calories from fat—3%; fat (gm)—less than 1 or 1% daily value; saturated fat (gm)—0; sodium (mg)—136; cholesterol (mg)—0; carbohydrates (gm)—37; dietary fiber (gm)—0; protein (gm)—0

Steamed Pearl Rice

Makes 2 cups or 4 (1/2-cup) servings

    1/4 teaspoon salt
    2/3 cup pearl, or short-grained, rice

Bring 1⅓ cups of water to a boil in a medium saucepan. Add the salt, stir in the rice, cover, and bring back to a boil. Reduce the heat to as low as possible and cook, covered, for 15 minutes without lifting the lid. Remove from the heat and let stand for at least 5 minutes or until you are ready to serve it.

Nutritional Profile per Serving: Calories—45; % calories from fat—10%; fat (gm)—less than 1 or 1% daily value; saturated fat (gm)—0; sodium (mg)—133; cholesterol (mg)—0; carbohydrates (gm)—10; dietary fiber (gm)—0; protein (gm)—0

Mixed Rice Vegetable Pilaf

Serves 4

1/2 teaspoon light olive oil with
    a dash of toasted sesame oil
1/2 teaspoon whole cumin seeds
1 cup mixed brown rice (I prefer Lundberg Jubilee)
2 cups low-sodium chicken stock (page 207)
    or vegetable stock (page 210) or water
1½ cups frozen peas and carrots

Bouquet Garni
3 cardamom pods
1-inch (2.5-cm) cinnamon stick
1 bay leaf
2 cloves
6 peppercorns

Heat a large saucepan over medium high heat. Pour in the oil and the cumin seeds and cook, stirring, until they darken, about 1 minute. Add the rice and stir until it begins to toast and pop. Pour in the stock or water and bring to a boil.

Tie the bouquet garni ingredients into a 6-inch (15-cm) square piece of cheese cloth and drop into the boiling stock. Cover and cook over very low heat for 20 minutes or until the rice is tender. Add the vegetables, cover, and let stand for 5 minutes off the heat. Remove the bouquet garni before serving.

Nutritional Profile per Serving: Calories—198; % calories from fat—9%; fat (gm)—2 or 3% daily value; saturated fat (gm)—0; sodium (mg)—34; cholesterol (mg)—0; carbohydrates (gm)—40; dietary fiber (gm)—4; protein (gm)—5

Swift Roasted Butternut Quarters

Serves 4

1 medium butternut squash, cut into quarters lengthwise, pulp removed

Preheat the oven to its highest setting: on "fan broil" for a convection oven or "bake" for a conventional oven. Lay the squash quarters on a rack in a broiler pan and roast, skin side up, for 25 minutes. These are wonderful served with a dollop of Yogurt Guacamole (page 128).

Nutritional Profile per Serving: Calories—68; % calories from fat—2%; fat (gm)—less than 1 or 1% daily value; saturated fat (gm)—0; sodium (mg)—7; cholesterol (mg)—0; carbohydrates (gm)—18; dietary fiber (gm)—5; protein (gm)—2

Shanghai Spinach Rice

Serves 4

1⅓ cups long-grain white rice
1/2 bunch spinach, rinsed and chopped (1 cup, loosely packed)
1/4 teaspoon Shanghai Coastline Ethmix (page 215)

Bring 6 cups of water to a boil in a saucepan. Stir in the rice, swirling around, and bring to a vigorous boil with the lid tipped. Remove the cover and maintain the boil for 10 minutes. Pour the rice and water through a strainer. Add fresh water to the saucepan and bring to a boil over high heat. Set the strainer of rice on top of the saucepan and cover. Reduce the heat to medium and steam for 10 minutes. Turn the heat to the lowest possible setting and thoroughly stir the chopped spinach and the seasoning mix into the rice in the strainer. Leave over very low heat until ready to serve.

Nutritional Profile per Serving: Calories—228; % calories from fat—2%; fat (gm)—less than 1 or 1% daily value; saturated fat (gm)—0; sodium (mg)—14; cholesterol (mg)—0; carbohydrates (gm)—50; dietary fiber (gm)—1; protein (gm)—5

Fruity Wild Rice

Serves 4

3 cups low-sodium chicken stock (page 207) or vegetable stock (page 210) or water
1/2 cup wild rice
1/2 cup long-grain brown rice
1/4 cup dried cranberries
4 green onions, chopped
1/2 teaspoon orange zest

Pour the stock or water into a large saucepan and stir in the wild rice. Bring to a boil and cook, covered, for 5 minutes. Add the brown rice, cover, and cook for 30 minutes or until the rice is as tender as you like it. Stir in the cranberries, chopped onion, and orange zest. Serve with turkey or pork.

Nutritional Profile per Serving: Calories—235; % calories from fat—6%; fat (gm)—2 or 2% daily value; saturated fat (gm)—0; sodium (mg)—38; cholesterol (mg)—0; carbohydrates (gm)—50; dietary fiber (gm)—3; protein (gm)—7

Grilled Sweet Potatoes

Serves 4

    2 sweet potatoes, cut in half lengthwise
    1/16 teaspoon salt
    1/16 teaspoon freshly ground black pepper

Preheat the electric grill to high or a gas grill to medium. If you are using a charcoal grill, do it with the indirect method where the hot charcoal lines the sides of the grill so the squash isn't subjected to its direct heat.

Dust each sweet potato half with salt and pepper. Lay the potato halves face down on the oiled grill for 15 minutes, then turn and cook 15 minutes longer or until tender.

Nutritional Profile per Serving: Calories—59; % calories from fat—8%; fat (gm)—less than 1 or 1% daily value; saturated fat (gm)—0; sodium (mg)—39; cholesterol (mg)—0; carbohydrates (gm)—14; dietary fiber (gm)—2; protein (gm)—0

Baked Russet Potato Halves

Serves 4

    2 large russet potatoes, scrubbed
    1 teaspoon freshly squeezed lemon juice
    1 teaspoon light olive oil with a dash of toasted sesame oil
    1/8 teaspoon salt
    1/8 teaspoon freshly ground black pepper

Preheat the convection oven to 350°F (180°C) or a conventional oven to 400°F (205°C).

Precook the potatoes in a microwave oven on high for 10 minutes, then cut in half lengthwise. Cut crossing diagonal lines into the potato flesh without breaking the skin, creating diamonds on each half. Mix the lemon juice and oil in a small bowl and brush on each potato half. Lightly dust with salt and pepper. Place the potatoes on a wire rack in a roasting pan and bake in the preheated convection oven for 15 minutes or in a conventional oven for 20 minutes.

Nutritional Profile per Serving: Calories—96; % calories from fat—11%; fat (gm)—1 or 2% daily value; saturated fat (gm)—0; sodium (mg)—71; cholesterol (mg)—0; carbohydrates (gm)—20; dietary fiber (gm)—1; protein (gm)—2

Swift Roasted Sweet Potato Spears

Serves 8

    8 very small sweet potatoes, cut in quarters lengthwise
    1 teaspoon light olive oil with a dash of toasted sesame oil
    1/4 teaspoon salt
    1/4 teaspoon ground white pepper
    1/2 teaspoon grated nutmeg

Preheat the oven to 450°F (230°C). Lay the sweet potato quarters on a rack in a roasting pan, brush with oil and sprinkle with salt, pepper, and nutmeg. Bake in a convection oven for 15 minutes or up to 25 minutes in a conventional oven.

Nutritional Profile per Serving: Calories—68; % calories from fat—9%; fat (gm)—less than 1 or 1% daily value; saturated fat (gm)—0; sodium (mg)—73; cholesterol (mg)—0; carbohydrates (gm)—15; dietary fiber (gm)—2; protein (gm)—1

The Bread Machine

Just like grandma used to make...

I'm not at all surprised to see the present bread revolution. It fits perfectly into our time-crazed, computerized, high-tech living that *craves* the "good old days" but just doesn't have time to put nostalgia into practice.

The bread machine is the darling of the housewares department and gourmet store. Especially popular are those you can load in the evening, set a time to coincide, like an aromatic orchestral suite, with the timer on the coffee machine, and "Jyan!" (pronounced jah-h-hn), which is Japanese for "Voilà!," you can spring out of bed to your very own Left Bank Café.

I tried some comparative tests with these machines and have decided it's really a matter of bells and whistles as to which (if any) you choose to buy. What I wanted to know was, which one would give me the equal of the best, real, crusty bread that I truly love to eat.

with bells and whistles

To my taste the Zojirushi S15A is the "upper crust" in a wide range of good machines, most of which do a great job. Whilst I'm fond of bells, I'm not so fond of whistles. The big thing is to buy only what you think you'll need.

regular bread machine

My unit of preference has a special program that allows me to set the time to bake my very own inventions as well as make jam, marmalade, apple butter, and cakes. To my mind, this spells out "individual creativity."

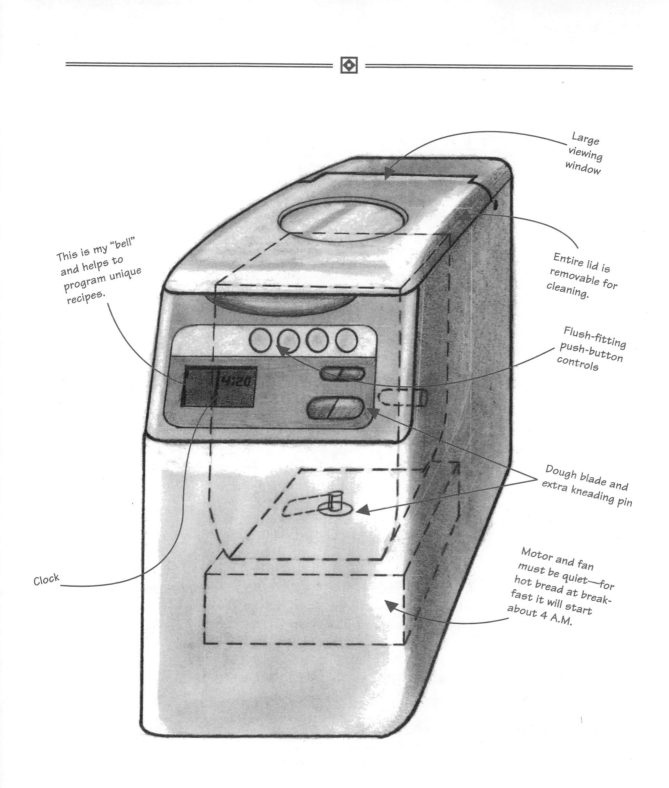

Large viewing window

Entire lid is removable for cleaning.

This is my "bell" and helps to program unique recipes.

Flush-fitting push-button controls

Dough blade and extra kneading pin

Clock

Motor and fan must be quiet—for hot bread at breakfast it will start about 4 A.M.

Focaccia

The dough for this focaccia (Italian flat bread) is prepared in a bread machine, then baked in a conventional oven. Bake it covered if you're going to make the grilled panini on page 42 or uncovered to eat on its own with soup or salad.

Serves 6

1 cup water
2 cups bread flour
1 packet active dry yeast (1 scant tablespoon)
1 tablespoon light olive oil with a dash of toasted sesame oil
2 cloves garlic, peeled, bashed, and chopped
1 teaspoon dried oregano
1/2 teaspoon fennel seeds

Place the ingredients in the bread machine pan in the order listed. Set the pan in the machine and follow the manufacturer's instructions for making dough. When the dough is ready (usually in about 1 hour 30 minutes), place it in an oiled bowl, cover with a clean cloth, and allow it to rise for 30 minutes. Preheat the oven to 375°F (190°C). Turn the dough out onto a greased 9 × 13-inch (23 × 33-cm) pan and pat it gently to flatten into a rectangle. Allow the dough to rest for 30 minutes, then dimple it all over by pressing firmly with your fingertips. Bake in the preheated oven 30 minutes or until golden brown.

To use for panini (page 42), cover the pan loosely with foil so the bread won't brown. The bottom will be golden; the top, springy to the touch.

To make focaccia by hand, start by dissolving the yeast in 1 cup of lukewarm water and letting it stand until creamy, about 10 minutes. Add the oil, stir, then beat in the garlic, oregano, fennel seeds, and enough of the flour to make a medium-firm dough. Turn out onto a lightly floured surface and knead for 10 minutes or until the dough is smooth and satiny. Place in an oiled bowl, cover with a towel, and let rise until double in size, about 1½ hours. Punch the dough down, let rise another 30 minutes, then follow the instructions for dimpling and baking above.

To serve: Cut each sandwich in half diagonally and serve on a plate with the Butter Lettuce and Arugula Salad (page 24).

Time Estimate: Preparation, 15 minutes; unsupervised, 2 hours 50 minutes

Nutritional Profile per Serving: Calories—224; % calories from fat—12%; fat (gm)—3 or 5% daily value; saturated fat (gm)—0; sodium (mg)—3; cholesterol (mg)—0; carbohydrates (gm)—42; dietary fiber (gm)—2; protein (gm)—8

Rustic French Bread

Makes 1 loaf (sixteen 1/2-inch or 1-cm slices)

1½ cups water
1 tablespoon honey
1/2 teaspoon salt
2½ cups white bread flour
3/4 cup whole wheat flour
1/4 cup rye flour
1½ teaspoons active dry yeast

To make the bread by machine: Place the ingredients in your bread machine pan in the order listed. Set the machine on the French bread setting and wait for a treat.

To make the bread by hand: Dissolve the yeast in 1/4 cup of lukewarm water and let it stand until creamy, about 10 minutes. Stir the remaining water and the honey together with the dissolved yeast. Whisk the flours and salt together and add the liquid. Mix with your hands or a wooden spoon until it forms a stiff dough and becomes a smooth ball. Knead for 10 minutes on a lightly floured board, then place in an oiled bowl, cover with a clean kitchen towel, and allow to double in size in a warm place, about 1½ hours. Shape into a disk on a flat cookie sheet covered with cornmeal. Cover lightly with a towel and let rise until double in size, about 1 hour.

Preheat the oven to 450°F (230°C). If you have a baking stone, set it in the center of the oven at the beginning of the preheating; if not, use another cookie sheet. Set an empty metal 8 × 8-inch (20 × 20-cm) baking pan on the bottom rack of the oven. When the dough and the oven are ready, place the unbaked loaf on the middle rack. Pour 2 cups of hot tap water into the hot pan underneath and quickly close the oven door. The water will make steam, which serves to make the crust nice and chewy. Bake until very dark brown, about 35 to 40 minutes. The interior temperature should be 190°F (88°C) or even a little higher when you stick an instant-read thermometer into the bottom of the loaf. Cool on a rack for at least an hour before slicing.

Time Estimate: Preparation, 10 minutes with bread machine or 30 minutes by hand; unsupervised, 4 hours 30 minutes with bread machine or 3 hours 40 minutes by hand

Nutritional Profile per Serving: Calories—101; % calories from fat—3%; fat (gm)—less than 1 or 1% daily value; saturated fat (gm)—0; sodium (mg)—68; cholesterol (mg)—0; carbohydrates (gm)—21; dietary fiber (gm)—2; protein (gm)—3

Rye Bread

Makes 1 loaf (sixteen 1/2-inch or 1-cm slices)

1/4 cup liquid egg substitute (I prefer Egg Beaters)
3/4 cup lukewarm water
1 tablespoon light olive oil with a dash of toasted sesame oil
1 tablespoon lemon juice
3 tablespoons molasses
1/4 teaspoon salt
1 tablespoon caraway seeds
2 tablespoons nonfat dry milk solids
1¼ cups white bread flour
1 cup whole wheat bread flour
3/4 cup rye flour
2 teaspoons active dry yeast

To make by machine: Place the ingredients in the order listed in the pan of your bread machine. Set it to Whole Wheat and start. In a little over 3 hours you will have a lovely loaf suitable for dinner, but especially good toasted for breakfast.

To make by hand: Dissolve the yeast in the warm water and let stand for 10 minutes. Add the egg substitute, oil, lemon juice, and molasses and stir. Mix the dry ingredients together in a large bowl and pour in the liquid. With your hands or a wooden spoon, combine to make a smooth dough. Knead for 10 minutes on a floured board, place in an oiled bowl, cover with a towel, and allow to rise until double in size, about 1½ hours. Punch the dough down, shape into a loaf, and place in an oiled 8½ × 4½ × 2½-inch (21 x 11 x 6-cm) loaf pan. Cover lightly with the towel and let rise until it's double in size, about another hour. Preheat the oven to 350°F (180°C). Bake the bread in the middle of the oven for 45 minutes or until an instant-read thermometer registers 190°F (88°C). Turn out of the pan and cool on a rack.

Time Estimate: Preparation, 10 minutes with a bread machine or 35 minutes by hand; unsupervised, 3 hours 28 minutes with a bread machine or 3 hours 15 minutes by hand

Nutritional Profile per Serving: Calories—107; % calories from fat—15%; fat (gm)—2 or 3% daily value; saturated fat (gm)—0; sodium (mg)—71; cholesterol (mg)—0; carbohydrates (gm)—20; dietary fiber (gm)—3; protein (gm)—4

Whole Wheat Quinoa Bread

Makes 1 loaf (sixteen 1/2-inch or 1-cm slices)

1¼ cups water
1 tablespoon light olive oil with a dash of toasted sesame oil
2 tablespoons honey
1/2 teaspoon salt
1¾ cups bread flour
1¾ cups whole wheat flour
1/3 cup uncooked quinoa
1¾ teaspoons active dry yeast

To make by machine: Place the ingredients in the order listed in your bread machine. Set it for Whole Wheat with a dark crust if you have that option.

To make by hand: Dissolve the yeast in 1/4 cup of lukewarm water and let stand for 10 minutes. Combine the remaining 1 cup of water, the oil, honey, and dissolved yeast in a small bowl. Combine the salt, bread flour, whole wheat flour, and quinoa in a large bowl. Pour the liquid into the dry ingredients and mix until you have a smooth ball. Knead for 10 minutes on a lightly floured board. Place the dough in a lightly oiled mixing bowl, cover with a clean kitchen towel, and let rise until double in volume, about 1½ hours. Punch the dough down, form into a loaf shape, and place in an oiled 9 × 5 × 3-inch loaf pan. Cover with the towel and let it rise again until double its original size, about 1 hour. Bake at 350°F (180°C) for 45 minutes to 1 hour or until an instant-read thermometer registers 190°F (88°C). Set on a rack to cool. Slice and enjoy!

Time Estimate: Preparation, 10 minutes with bread machine or 25 minutes by hand; unsupervised, 3 hours 50 minutes with bread machine or 3 hours 15 minutes by hand

Nutritional Profile per Serving: Calories—124;% calories from—10%; fat (gm)—1 or 2% daily value; saturated fat (gm)—0; sodium (mg)—69; cholesterol (mg)—0; carbohydrates (gm)—25; dietary fiber (gm)—2; protein (gm)—4

Desserts

The Ice Cream Maker

when you're through there...

Several years ago, we got the Donvier ice cream maker. A simple brine-filled, metal-jacketed sleeve whose contents could be frozen solid in 6 to 12 hours. Then, like its brass-bound parent, you inserted the churning handle and tried to remember every 10 minutes or so to give it a few cranks. It was so simple and very effective.

Anything that can be turned by hand will eventually be motorized. It happened to the Model T Ford, and now the Donvier idea has been powered up to relieve us busy people from the ordeal of turning a handle a couple of dozen times. Krups has given us La Glacière, an ice cream maker with a motor but without the fuss of ice and salt. I find this machine to be a great help in achieving smooth and creamy low-fat frozen yogurts and sorbets.

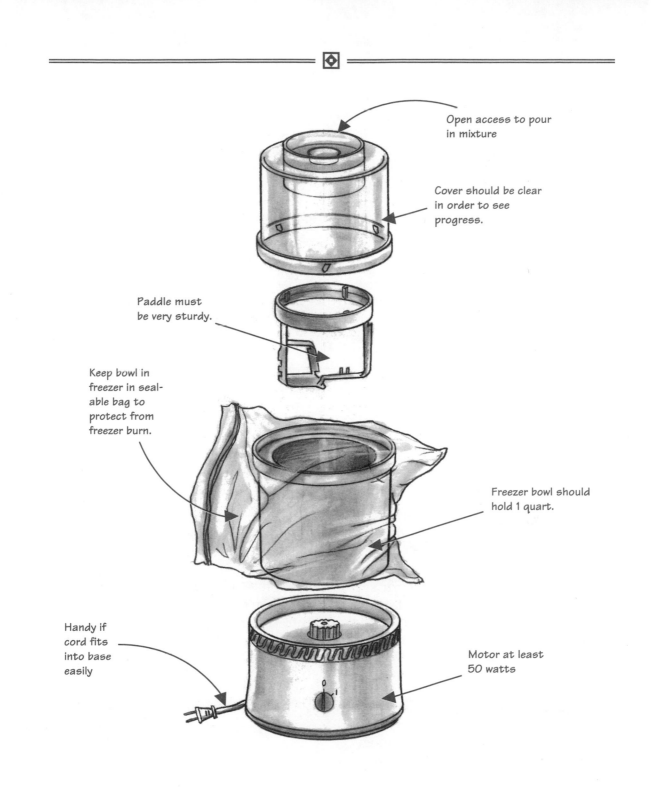

Open access to pour in mixture

Cover should be clear in order to see progress.

Paddle must be very sturdy.

Keep bowl in freezer in sealable bag to protect from freezer burn.

Freezer bowl should hold 1 quart.

Handy if cord fits into base easily

Motor at least 50 watts

Cinnamon Apple Frozen Yogurt

I've discovered that soy milk helps to smooth out homemade frozen yogurt. This recipe and the Raspberry Pavlova with Berry Sauce that follows have the best texture I've achieved to date. Please try them and let me know what you think.

Makes 1 quart

2 medium cooking apples (Jonagold,
    Gravenstein, Winesap), peel on,
    roughly chopped
1 cup de-alcoholized white zinfandel
1 tablespoon cornstarch mixed with 2 tablespoons de-alcoholized white zinfandel (slurry)
1/4 cup sugar
1/4 cup light corn syrup
1/4 teaspoon ground cinnamon
1/4 teaspoon vanilla
1 cup yogurt cheese (page 210)
3/4 cup 1% soy milk

Cook the chopped apples with the wine over medium heat until the apples are very soft and the liquid is almost gone, about 25 minutes. Push through a strainer, pressing to get all the apple pulp; discard the debris left in the strainer. Return the strained purée to the saucepan, stir in the slurry, and heat to cook the cornstarch, 30 seconds to 1 minute. Add the sugar, corn syrup, cinnamon, and vanilla, stirring until the sugar is dissolved. Allow to cool, then set in the refrigerator to chill.

Whisk the yogurt and soy milk together until very smooth. Add the chilled apple mixture and stir until well mixed. Pour into your ice cream freezer and freeze according to the manufacturer's directions. Let it ripen in the freezer for 1 hour if you like. It is best served slightly soft.

Time Estimate: Preparation, 10 minutes; cooking, 26 minutes; unsupervised, 20 minutes

Nutritional Profile per Serving*

	Apple Cinnamon Frozen Yogurt	Classic Apple Cinnamon Ice Cream
Calories	241	447
Fat (gm)	1	39
% Daily value of fat	1%	60%
Saturated fat (gm)	0	24
Calories from fat	3%	79%
Cholesterol (mg)	2	145
Sodium (mg)	141	70
Fiber (gm)	2	0
Carbohydrates (gm)	53	24
Protein (gm)	8	2

* I am giving you a comparison because full-fat ice creams make a substantial contribution to overall fat consumption. This could help you decide upon a very swiftly made, almost fat-free treat.

Raspberry Pavlova with Berry Sauce

Serves 6

Meringue
2 large egg whites
1/8 teaspoon cream of tartar
1/4 cup superfine sugar (see Note)
1/8 teaspoon almond extract

Frozen yogurt
2 (12-ounce or 340-gm) packages frozen raspberries
2 tablespoons cornstarch mixed with 1/4 cup raspberry juice (slurry)
1/4 cup sugar
1/4 cup light corn syrup
1/2 teaspoon vanilla
1 tablespoon freshly squeezed lemon juice
1 cup yogurt cheese (page 210)
3/4 cup 1% fat soy milk

Sauce
2 cups frozen mixed berries (blueberries, raspberries, strawberries, and blackberries)
2 tablespoons sugar
1/2 teaspoon arrowroot mixed with 1 teaspoon water (slurry)

Garnish
4 fresh mint sprigs or edible flowers

Preheat the oven to 225°F (95°C).

For the meringue: Beat the egg whites until foamy; add the cream of tartar and continue beating until soft peaks form. Sprinkle the sugar in gradually while continuing to beat until stiff peaks form. Fold in the almond extract last. Spoon the meringue into a pastry bag with a medium-size (Ateco #3) tip. Cover a baking sheet with parchment paper. Create small cups in this manner: Pipe meringue in a coil, starting in the middle and moving out in concentric circles to form the bottom. Three circles piped one atop the other around the outside edge will form the sides. You should have enough meringue to make six 3-inch cups. Bake in the preheated oven for 2 hours or until dry but not brown. Store in an airtight container until you are ready to use.

For the frozen yogurt: Thaw the raspberries and press through a sieve. You should get 1½ cups of raspberry juice. Reserve 1/4 cup of the juice for the slurry and pour the rest into a saucepan. Bring to a boil and cook until reduced to 1 cup, which will take about 10 minutes. Remove from the heat to add the slurry, then return to the heat to cook the cornstarch until clear, for 30 seconds to 1 minute. Stir in the sugar, corn syrup, vanilla, and lemon juice. Set in the refrigerator to chill.

Stir the yogurt and soy milk together with a wire whisk until there are no lumps. Add the chilled raspberry syrup and stir until well mixed. Pour into your ice cream freezer and follow the manufacturer's directions. This will take about 20 minutes in most electric machines. Let ripen for an hour in the freezer.

To make the sauce: Thaw the mixed berries and press through a sieve into a small saucepan. Add the sugar and slurry. Heat, stirring often to dissolve the sugar and thicken the sauce.

To serve: Set a meringue cup filled with raspberry frozen yogurt onto each of 6 dessert plates. Spoon the sauce around each meringue and garnish with a sprig of fresh mint or an edible flower such as a pansy.

Note: I make my own superfine sugar by simply whizzing granulated sugar in my blender until it's a powdery consistency. Don't substitute confectioners' sugar, because it contains cornstarch, which would toughen the meringue.

Time Estimate: Preparation, 30 minutes; cooking, 25 minutes; unsupervised, 3 hours

Nutritional Profile per Serving: Calories—266; % calories from fat—4%; fat (gm)—1 or 2% daily value; saturated fat (gm)—0; sodium (mg)—102; cholesterol (mg)—1; carbohydrates (gm)—60; dietary fiber (gm)—6; protein (gm)—7

Fruit on Fruit

Y ou are now about to set sail on a sea of potential elegance. To my mind, palate, and experience, nothing can beat the extraordinary delicacy of properly cooked, spiced, and partnered fruit.

For each of the twenty-seven different fruits, I've suggested the name of a good variety, when it's available on a national basis, and the season when it should be in ready supply. Also, I've included suggestions for cooking methods (which are more fully discussed at the end of the list) and the results of our experiments using Ariél de-alcoholized wines as a cooking medium. You may, of course, choose Ariél or wines with alcohol according to your personal preference. When alcohol is added to a dish, the number of calories will rise. The dessert with alcohol may not be suitable for, or enjoyed by, children and the seasoning will need to be more robust in order to balance the alcohol "burn."

As of the date of publication, I need to explain that not all de-alcoholized wines are acceptable in these recipes because different production methods are used with varying degrees of success. I use Ariél brand as my standard of quality.

I have also reviewed the world of spices and suggested several that will react like nuclear fusion where *one plus one equals two point three*. It's the flavor combinations that become more than the sum of the two ingredients and explode in your mouth! You will find sauce suggestions and will be able to select from your own basic recipes or mine that follow.

Finally, I've listed companion fruits that you might like to present as a team. All in all, you have a *minimum* of five variations for each of the twenty-seven fruits, or at least one hundred and thirty-five ideas!

However you choose to mix and match, you'll be reducing the health risks from the types of desserts that you literally have to die for! Here are the basic techniques to help you on your way. In every case the fruit desserts can be served from pan to plate hot or allowed to cool and served chilled.

27 varieties!
5 or more companion fruits!
135 ideas !!!

Cooking with Fruit

Apples

Varieties—Jonagold, Gravenstein (eating/cooking), Rome, Winesap, McIntosh (best cooking)
Season—available year round, peak August through November
Cooking techniques—braise, bake, sauté
Cooking liquids—de-alcoholized white zinfandel, apple juice
Spices—cinnamon, allspice
Sauce—custard, caramel
Companion fruits—cranberry, rhubarb

Apricots

Variety—Tilton
Season—July through September
Cooking techniques—poach, smooth sauce
Cooking liquid—de-alcoholized white zinfandel
Spices—cardamom, cloves
Sauce—fruit
Companion fruits—papaya, pineapple

Asian Pears (Nashi)

Variety—Twentieth Century
Season—July through March
Cooking techniques—poach, sauté
Cooking liquid—sparkling white de-alcoholized wine
Spices—allspice, cinnamon
Sauce—chocolate, fruit
Companion fruits—banana, mango

Bananas

Variety—Cavendish
Season—available year round
Cooking techniques—sauté
Cooking liquid—de-alcoholized white zinfandel
Spices—allspice, cardamom, cinnamon, cloves
Sauce—chocolate
Companion fruits—raspberry, pineapple

Blackberries

Variety—Ollalie (sweet), Marion (tart)
Season—June through September
Cooking techniques—sauce, ice
Cooking liquid—sparkling white wine
Spices—cinnamon, nutmeg
Sauce—custard
Companion fruits—other berries, banana, peach

Blueberries

Variety—Bluecrop
Season—June through August
Cooking techniques—sauce, in low-fat pastry
Cooking liquid—sparkling white wine
Spices—cinnamon, ginger
Sauce—custard, fruit
Companion fruits—other berries, cranberry

Cherries

Variety—sour cherries (best cooking), Bing, Rainer (best eating)
Season—June through August
Cooking techniques—poach, sweet soup, sweet or savory
    sauce, braise
Cooking liquid—Champagne or sparkling white de-alcoholized
    wine
Spices—cardamom, ginger
Sauce—custard
Companion fruits—orange, banana

Cranberries

Variety—McFarlin
Season—September through December
Cooking techniques—braise, boil, ice
Cooking liquid—white zinfandel wine, apple juice
Spices—cinnamon, ginger
Sauce—fruit
Companion fruits—oranges, green grapes

Dates

Variety—Deglet Noor (best cooking), Medjool (best eating)
Season—year round
Cooking techniques—garnish in sweet or savory dishes
Cooking liquid—de-alcoholized white zinfadel
Spices—ginger, allspice
Sauce—fruit
Companion fruits—mango, orange

Figs

Variety—White Kadota (cooking),
    White Calmyrna (eating)
Season—July through October
Cooking techniques—poach, macerate
Cooking liquid—de-alcoholized fruity white wine
Spices—allspice, cinnamon, ginger, nutmeg
Sauce—fruit
Companion fruits—apricot, mango

Grapefruit

Variety—Texas Pink
Season—January through April
Cooking techniques—ice, broil
Cooking liquid—sparkling white de-alcoholized
    wine or Champagne
Spices—mint
Sauce—custard, fruit
Companion fruits—strawberries, grapes

Grapes

Variety—Thompson seedless, green or flame, red
Season—June through March with a summer peak
Cooking techniques—macerate, poach
Cooking liquid—sparkling white de-alcoholized wine or
    Champagne
Spices—cinnamon, ginger
Sauce—fruit, yogurt, custard
Companion fruits—kiwi, mango

Kiwifruit

Variety—Hayward
Season—June through March
Cooking techniques—best used raw, macerate
Cooking liquid—de-alcoholized blanc
Spices—allspice, cardamom
Sauce—custard, yogurt, fruit
Companion fruits—mango, banana

Lychees

Variety—Brewster, Mauritius
Season—canned, year round; fresh, July
Cooking techniques—macerate, poach
Cooking liquid—sparkling white de-alcoholized wine or
    champagne
Spices—ginger, cardamom
Sauce—fruit
Companion fruits—Asian pear, papaya

Mangoes

Variety—Tommy Atkins
Season—January through August
Cooking techniques—braise, reduction sauce
Cooking liquid—sparkling white de-alcoholized wine or
    Champagne
Spices—cardamom, nutmeg
Sauce—fruit, custard
Companion fruits—papaya, pineapple

Melons

Variety—cantaloupe, honeydew
Season—July through October
Cooking techniques—best not cooked, macerate, salad
Cooking liquid—sparkling white de-alcoholized
    wine or Champagne
Spices—cardamom, nutmeg
Sauce—fruit
Companion fruits—kiwi, grapes

Nectarines

Variety—Summer Grand
Season—May through September
Cooking techniques—poach, sauce
Cooking liquid—de-alcoholized fruity white wine
Spices—nutmeg, allspice
Sauce—custard
Companion fruits—banana, raspberry

Oranges

Variety—Navel (eating), Valencia (juice), Seville (marmalade)
Season—Navels, November through May; Valencias, year
    round; Seville, January and February
Cooking techniques—macerate, salads, ice
Cooking liquid—de-alcoholized white zinfandel
Spices—mint
Sauce—custard, chocolate
Companion fruits—grapes, nectarines

Papayas

Variety—Solo
Season—available year round, peak May and October
Cooking techniques—sauce with arrowroot
Cooking liquid—de-alcoholized, fruity white wine or
    sparkling white de-alcoholized wine
Spices—cinnamon, cardamom
Sauce—fruit
Companion fruits—banana, strawberry

Peaches

Variety—Redhaven, Fairhaven, Elberta, Sunhaven (clingstone)
Season—May through September, peaks July and August
Cooking techniques—poach, broil, bake
Cooking liquid—sparkling white de-alcoholized wine or
    Champagne
Spices—allspice, cinnamon, nutmeg
Sauce—custard, yogurt
Companion fruits—apricots, raspberries

Pears

Variety—Bosc (cooking), Bartlett or Comice (eating)
Season—July through March
Cooking techniques—poach, steam, ice, braise
Cooking liquid—sparkling white de-alcoholized wine,
    Champagne, spicy syrup
Spices—ginger, cinnamon
Sauce—chocolate, custard, fruit
Companion fruits—cranberry, apricot

Pineapples

Variety—Sugar Loaf, Red Spanish
Season—available year round, peaks April through June
Cooking techniques—broil, bake, ice
Cooking liquid—de-alcoholized sparkling white wine or white zinfandel
Spices—cardamom, ginger
Sauce—custard, fruit
Companion fruits—grapes, blueberries, apricots

Plums

Variety—Santa Rosa, Italian Prune
Season—May through September
Cooking techniques—braise, bake, as a dessert sauce or
    sauce for meat
Cooking liquid—de-alcoholized fruity white wine
Spices—cardamom, cinnamon
Sauce—fruit
Companion fruits—blackberries, pears

Prunes

Variety—d'Agen Prune
Season—available year round
Cooking techniques—poach
Cooking liquid—de-alcoholized fruity white wine
Spices—cinnamon, ginger
Sauce—fruit
Companion fruits—apple, Asian pear

Raspberries

Variety—Meeker
Season—June through September
Cooking techniques—sauce, ice
Cooking liquid—de-alcoholized fruity white wine
Spices—cardamom, cinnamon
Sauce—custard, chocolate
Companion fruits—other berries, mango

Rhubarb

Variety—Crimson Rhubarb
Season—April through June
Cooking techniques—braise, sauce
Cooking liquid—de-alcoholized white zinfandel
Spices—a touch of cinnamon
Sauce—custard, fruit
Companion fruits—blueberry, orange

Strawberries

Variety—Selva
Season—early summer
Cooking techniques—sauce, ice
Cooking liquid—sparkling white de-alcoholized
    wine or Champagne
Spices—cinnamon, mint
Sauce—yogurt, custard
Companion fruits—rhubarb, dates, other berries

Basic Fruit Preparation Methods

Sauté

The oil should be neutral in flavor, such as the extra light (refers to flavor) flavorless olive oil. Then you can add a few drops of toasted sesame seed oil for a nutty flavor. I use very little—one teaspoonful of oil for a four-portion dessert.

Heat the oil in a skillet and add fruit that has been cut into one-inch-thick slices or wedges. Sprinkle with a little ground spice, using no more than one-sixteenth teaspoonful per panful of fruit and one tablespoon of sugar (depending on the fruit to be served, of course).

Set on a moderate heat to steam through and let the sweet juices mingle and caramelize when sufficiently concentrated. Serve these simple sautés with frozen low-fat yogurt, spooned over a slice of angel food cake, or wrapped in a thin pancake or crêpe.

Poach

When poaching, you must rely upon a beautifully seasoned pool of cooking liquid being brought up to the boil while never being allowed to actually bubble. In this very hot bath, the fruit will gently relax as the internal temperatures rise and force its natural juices out to mingle with the hot liquid. When the heat is turned down, the juices return to the fruit and the miracle of multiplied flavors begins.

The poaching liquid can be totally or partly created from wine or clear fruit juices, or a blend. My personal preference is to use de-alcoholized wines, and I recommend Ariél brands. Finely grated citrus zests (orange, grapefruit, lime, tangerine) can be added to the liquid but, for my taste, must be removed before serving.

When the peeled and sliced fruit is perfectly cooked, lift it from the liquid and keep it warm. Strain the liquid and return it to a saucepan to be thickened with a little cornstarch or arrowroot (one tablespoon to each one cup of liquid) mixed first into a slurry with cold juices. Then bring the sauce to a boil for 30 seconds to clear the starchy taste of the cornstarch (this is unnecessary when using arrowroot).

Please try it then, and add a little sugar or freshly squeezed lemon juice according to taste and *maybe* a touch more of a warm, aromatic spice such as cloves, cinnamon, nutmeg, allspice, or cardamom. Coat the fruit with the sauce and serve it hot over cold rice pudding or just as it is.

Broil (radiant overhead heat)

Peel and core or pit the fruit and brush lightly with melted brown sugar, seasoned to your liking with warming spices. Place on a nonstick baking pan so that the tops of the fruit are about 4 inches (10 cm) from the heat source. Cook until just lightly browned.

I like to serve broiled fruit with a sprig of cool, fresh green mint and wedges of orange or lemon on the side, with perhaps a couple of gingersnap cookies.

Bake

This method produces much the same result as broiling, but obviously takes a little longer and permits larger pieces to be more evenly cooked. It has the added benefit of not having to be watched all the time.

Oven temperatures should be 350°F (180°C) for juicy fruit and 425°F for apricots, pears, and peaches. Baking times run from 30 minutes down to 20 minutes for fruit with a higher sugar content.

A baste can be made with reduced de-alcoholized wine, brown sugar, and one of the warming spices. As always, please be restrained with the amount of spice added.

Braise

This is a poaching process that takes place in the oven. The fruit is almost covered with the poaching liquid and baked at 350°F (180°C) for 30 minutes or until tender. As with poaching, the juices can be thickened and warmly seasoned to taste.

Smooth Sauces

All fruit can be made into smooth sauces. Some need an extra sieving to eliminate seeds or fiber, but otherwise all can be poached until very tender and then puréed (whizzed) in a blender along with a small amount of the cooking liquid.

My "sock 'n sieve" and strainer (see below) will help to swiftly remove seeds and fiber.

In some cases you may need to add a little arrowroot slurry, one tablespoon for each one cup of liquid. Arrowroot brings a brilliantly clear gloss to the sauce and seems to brighten the color without obscuring the taste.

Please buy arrowroot by the one-pound packet in health food stores or food co-operatives and not in small, expensive glass jars.

For custard-style sauces that are low in fat and calories, all you need to do is gently stir in low-fat vanilla yogurt. You can also blend dense poached fruit such as pears, bananas, apples, apricots, or peaches with unsweetened evaporated skim milk in the ratio of 8 fluid ounces (1 cup) for each one pound of fruit and sweeten to taste.

Macerate

This is an almost out-of-date term that needs to be revived. It comes from the French *macéérer*, to place fruit in a liquid to absorb or give off flavor. I macerate fruit in de-alcoholized wines that I have reduced by half, in order to concentrate their flavor. After the fruit has soaked overnight I take a third of the volume and sieve it to produce a purée. I use this as a sauce for the remaining macerated fruit.

Fruit Ices

Many of the fruits mentioned can be made into a frozen dessert. You can make a triple batch when poaching, baking, braising, or shallow frying and let the fruit cool in its extra cooking juices. Whiz it in a blender until smooth; pour into a tray and partially freeze. Then whip the slush to beat air into it and return to the freezer.

You can use this same fruit purée in the ice cream machines described on pages 176–177 with really excellent results.

Sautéed Nashi in Crispy Cups

Serves 4

Cups
4 egg roll wrappers
1 teaspoon sugar

Cream filling
1/4 cup low-fat vanilla yogurt
1 teaspoon chopped crystallized ginger

Sautéed nashi filling
3 (1½-pound or 681-gm) Asian pears or nashi, peeled, cored, and cut into twelfths
1/16 teaspoon ground ginger
1 tablespoon sugar
1 tablespoon chopped crystallized ginger
1 tablespoon lemon juice
1 teaspoon light olive oil with a dash of sesame oil

Garnish
1 teaspoon toasted sesame seeds

To make the cups: Preheat the oven to 350°F (180°C). Lay the egg roll wrappers on the kitchen bench and spray lightly with olive oil cooking spray. Sprinkle with sugar. Tuck each wrapper into a large-cup muffin tin and bake for 5 minutes. Remove from the oven, take the partially baked wrappers out of the muffin cups, turn the muffin tin over and place the partially baked wrappers over the back of the muffin cups. Bake for 3 more minutes or until evenly brown and crisp. (Bake extras if you like, as they keep well in an airtight container.) Set aside to cool.

For the cream filling: Mix the yogurt and ginger together in a small bowl and set aside.

For the sautéed nashi filling: Toss the nashi slices, ground ginger, sugar, crystallized ginger, and lemon juice together to coat the slices. Heat the oil in a skillet over medium high heat. Fry the nashi, stirring and shaking the pan, until they are tender and the sugar has caramelized, about 10 minutes.

To serve: Spoon 1 tablespoon of the yogurt cream into each of the cups. Fill with the sautéed nashi and sprinkle with toasted sesame seeds.

Time Estimate: Preparation, 15 minutes; cooking, 18 minutes

Nutritional Profile per Serving: Calories—123; % calories from fat—7%; fat (gm)—1 or 2% daily value; saturated fat (gm)—0; sodium (mg)—62; cholesterol (mg)—1; carbohydrates (gm)—27; dietary fiber (gm)—4; protein (gm)—2

Bananas with Pineapple Sauce

Serves 4

Sauce
1½ cups fresh pineapple chunks
1 teaspoon freshly squeezed lemon juice
1 tablespoon honey

Bananas
1 teaspoon light olive oil with a dash of sesame oil
4 medium bananas, peeled and cut on the diagonal into thick slices
1/8 teaspoon ground cardamom
1/2 cup vanilla yogurt cheese (page 210)

For the sauce: Place the pineapple, lemon juice, and honey in a blender and whiz for 1 minute.

For the bananas: Heat the oil in a nonstick skillet over medium high heat. Place the banana slices in the hot pan, sprinkle with cardamom, and fry until golden, about 2½ minutes per side.

To serve: Place 2 tablespoons of the yogurt cheese into each of 4 dessert bowls. Divide the hot bananas among bowls and top with the pineapple sauce. Serve immediately. This dish could also be served in egg-roll wrapper cups found on page 193.

Time Estimate: Preparation, 15 minutes; cooking, 5 minutes

Nutritional Profile per Serving: Calories—211; % calories from fat—13%; fat (gm)—3 or 5% daily value; saturated fat (gm)—1; sodium (mg)—42; cholesterol (mg)—3; carbohydrates (gm)—47; dietary fiber (gm)—3; protein (gm)—4

Poached Rhubarb Sauce
with Blueberries over Orange Sections

Serves 4

1 pound (454 gm) rhubarb, trimmed and cut into thin slices
1/4 cup orange juice
5 tablespoons sugar
1/2 teaspoon finely grated orange zest
1 cup fresh or frozen blueberries
2 large navel oranges, peeled and cut into sections

Garnish
4 sprigs fresh mint

Combine the rhubarb, orange juice, sugar, and orange zest in a saucepan. Cover, bring to a boil over medium high heat, then turn to low and cook for 8 minutes or until the rhubarb is very soft. Stir in the blueberries and chill for later, or spoon into 4 dessert bowls. Arrange the orange sections in a flower shape on top of the sauce and garnish with a sprig of mint.

Time Estimate: Preparation, 20 minutes; cooking, 8 minutes

Nutritional Profile per Serving: Calories—150; % calories from fat—0%; fat (gm)—0 or 0% daily value; saturated fat (gm)—0; sodium (mg)—6; cholesterol (mg)—0; carbohydrates (gm)—38; dietary fiber (gm)—4; protein (gm)—2

Spicy Apple Torte

Soy milk smooths this sauce to the texture of a good crème anglaise. The yogurt loses any chalkiness, just leaving the tanginess to be tamed by the maple syrup. What a combination!

Serves 4

1 cup clear unsweetened apple juice
1/4 teaspoon cinnamon
1/8 teaspoon allspice
1/8 teaspoon ground red pepper (cayenne) (optional)
1 tablespoon freshly squeezed lemon juice
4 cooking apples (McIntosh, Jonagold, Winesap), peeled, cored, and thinly sliced
2 tablespoons dried cranberries
16 savoiardi (Italian crisp ladyfingers)
1½ teaspoons arrowroot mixed with 1 tablespoon apple juice (slurry)

Sauce
1 cup yogurt cheese (page 210)
1/4 cup light soy milk
2 tablespoons pure maple syrup
1/2 teaspoon vanilla

Garnish
1 tablespoon dried cranberries
2 tablespoons toasted chopped walnuts

> Savoiardi are wonderful crisp Italian ladyfingers made by a company called Ferrara. They are very low in fat, and they have a good texture and a mild, sweet flavor. You should be able to find them in an Italian grocery or a large food chain. It will be worth the search!

Preheat the oven to 350°F (180°C). Combine the apple juice, cinnamon, allspice, cayenne, and lemon juice in a medium saucepan and bring to a boil. Drop the sliced apples into the hot liquid and poach for 5 to 10 minutes (depending on the apple) or until the apples are soft but not mushy. Add the cranberries when the apples are cooked. Drain through a sieve, reserving the liquid. Lay 8 ladyfingers across the bottom of a lightly greased 9 × 5 × 2½-inch (23½ × 13 × 6-cm) loaf pan. It won't hurt if they are a little crowded. Spoon the cooked apples onto the ladyfingers, pressing gently, and lay the rest of the ladyfingers over the top. Cover loosely with aluminum foil and bake 15 minutes.

While the torte is baking, pour the poaching liquid back into the poaching pan, add the slurry, and stir gently over the heat to clear and thicken. Set aside.

For the sauce: Combine all the sauce ingredients and stir with a wire whisk until perfectly smooth.

To serve: When the apple torte is ready, run a knife around the edges, lay a serving platter over the top, and tip the torte onto the platter, being careful not to burn yourself on the hot pan. Pour the thickened poaching liquid around the sides of the torte, lifting it gently to allow the liquid to run underneath. Spoon some of the yogurt sauce down the middle of the torte and top with cranberries and walnuts. Cut into 4 pieces and pass the remaining yogurt sauce.

Time Estimate: Preparation, 25 minutes; cooking, 12 minutes; unsupervised, 15 minutes

Nutritional Profile per Serving: Calories—188; % calories from fat—10%; fat (gm)—2 or 3% daily value; saturated fat (gm)—0; sodium (mg)— 74; cholesterol (mg)—8; carbohydrates (gm)—42; dietary fiber (gm)— 2; protein (gm)—4

Broiled Apricots with Almonds

Serves 4

4 teaspoons brown sugar
1/4 teaspoon ground cardamom
8 plump fresh apricots, pitted and halved
4 teaspoons sliced almonds
2 cups low-fat frozen yogurt

Preheat the broiler in your oven. Combine the brown sugar and cardamom in a small bowl. Spread the apricot halves on a work surface, pit side up. Sprinkle with the sugar and spice mixture and top with the almonds. Set on a broiler pan and place about 6 inches (15 cm) from the heat source. Broil until the sugar bubbles and the almonds turn brown, 2 to 5 minutes depending on your broiler. Watch carefully—the almonds can turn black and bitter in the wink of an eye.

Spoon the frozen yogurt into 4 small bowls and flatten with your spoon. Place the hot apricots on top and serve.

Time Estimate: Preparation, 15 minutes; cooking, 5 minutes

Nutritional Profile per Serving: Calories—160; % calories from fat—17%; fat (gm)—3 or 5% daily value; saturated fat (gm)—1; sodium (mg)—61; cholesterol (mg)—5; carbohydrates (gm)—30; dietary fiber (gm)—1; protein (gm)—6

Strawberry Broiled Grapefruit

Serves 4

   2 large pink grapefruit, cut in half
   8 teaspoons strawberry jam
   1 tablespoon chopped fresh mint
   2 large fresh strawberries, cut in half lengthwise

Preheat the broiler in your oven. Spread the 4 grapefruit halves with jam and set on a broiler pan. Place about 4 inches (10 cm) from the heat source and broil until the jam starts to bubble and darken, 3 to 5 minutes depending on your broiler.

Sprinkle the mint over the tops of the grapefruit halves and lay a strawberry half in the center of each one. Serve immediately.

Time Estimate: Preparation, 10 minutes; cooking, 5 minutes

Nutritional Profile per Serving: Calories—100; % calories from fat—0%; fat (gm)—0 or 0% daily value; saturated fat (gm)—0; sodium (mg)—26; cholesterol (mg)—0; carbohydrates (gm)—23; dietary fiber (gm)—4; protein (gm)—3

Baked Ginger Pineapple

Serves 4

   1 fresh pineapple, topped, quartered, core removed
   4 tablespoons finely chopped crystallized ginger

Preheat the oven to 350°F (180°C). Run a knife blade between the flesh and skin of each pineapple quarter, leaving the flesh sitting on the skin. Slice the flesh crosswise at about 1/2-inch (1.25-cm) intervals, then make one cut lengthwise from end to end. This will leave you with bite-size chunks. Sprinkle the crystallized ginger over the top, Place in a glass baking dish and bake in the preheated oven for 20 minutes or until heated through. Serve warm.

Time Estimate: Preparation; 15 minutes; unsupervised, 20 minutes

Nutritional Profile per Serving: Calories—125; % calories from fat—7%; fat (gm)—1 or 2% daily value; saturated fat (gm)—0; sodium (mg)—18; cholesterol (mg)—0; carbohydrates (gm)—31; dietary fiber (gm)—2; protein (gm)—0

Baked Peach Slices

Serves 4

1 cup fruity white wine
1/4 cup packed brown sugar
6 whole allspice or 1/8 teaspoon ground allspice
1 tablespoon lemon juice
4 peaches, peeled, pitted, and cut into 1/2-inch (1.25-cm) slices

Garnish
2 tablespoons toasted sliced almonds (optional)

Preheat the oven to 425°F (220°C). Mix the wine, brown sugar, allspice, and lemon juice in a saucepan and bring to a rapid boil. Boil to reduce the liquid by half, which will take 5 to 10 minutes. Lay the peach slices in an 8 × 8-inch (20 × 20-cm) glass baking dish. Pour the reduced basting liquid over the top and bake, uncovered, in the preheated oven for 20 minutes or until tender but not mushy. If your peaches are ripe and in season, you should probably check them for tenderness after 10 or 15 minutes. Remove the allspice berries if you used them.

You may eat the baked peaches hot or cold as they are, with the almonds sprinkled over the top, or as a garnish topping for low-fat frozen yogurt, angel food cake, or wrapped in a crêpe (page 214).

Time Estimate: Preparation, 10 minutes; cooking, 10 minutes; unsupervised, 20 minutes

Nutritional Profile per Serving: Calories—204; % calories from fat—9%; fat (gm)—2 or 3% daily value; saturated fat (gm)—0; sodium (mg)—8; cholesterol (mg)—0; carbohydrates (gm)—48; dietary fiber (gm)—6; protein (gm)—3. Profile includes the almonds.

Tropical Fruit Compote

Serves 6

1/2 fresh pineapple, peeled, cored, and cut into
    1-inch (2.5-cm) chunks
1 papaya, peeled, seeded, and cut into 1-inch (2.5-cm) chunks
1 mango, peeled and cut into 1/2-inch (1.25-cm) slices
3 plums, pitted and cut into eighths
1 cup fruity medium-dry white wine

2 tablespoons lemon juice
1/4 cup packed brown sugar
1/4 teaspoon ground cardamom
1 tablespoon arrowroot mixed with
    2 tablespoons de-alcoholized
    white wine (slurry)

Preheat the oven to 350°F (180°C). Mix the fruit pieces in a glass baking dish. Combine the wine, lemon juice, brown sugar, and cardamom in a small bowl and stir until the sugar is dissolved. Pour over the fruit. Bake, uncovered, for 30 minutes in the preheated oven or until the pineapple is tender but still holds its shape. Carefully pour the liquid into a saucepan, stir in the slurry, and heat until the sauce clears and thickens. Pour back into the fruit. The compote may be served warm or cold, on its own, or over frozen yogurt or rice pudding.

Time Estimate: Preparation, 20 minutes; unsupervised, 30 minutes

Nutritional Profile per Serving: Calories—111; % calories from fat—8%; fat (gm)—1 or 2% daily value; saturated fat (gm)—0; sodium (mg)—8; cholesterol (mg)—0; carbohydrates (gm)—28; dietary fiber (gm)—3; protein (gm)—1

Sparkling Melon with Strawberries

Serves 6

1/2 cantaloupe, peeled and cut into 1-inch (2.5-cm) chunks
1/2 honeydew melon, peeled and cut into 1-inch (2.5-cm) chunks
12 large strawberries, stemmed and cut in half
1 teaspoon lime zest
2 cups fruity medium-dry sparkling wine

Place the fruit in a glass bowl, sprinkle with the lime zest, and pour the sparkling wine over the top. Chill for at least 2 hours. Serve in chilled wine glasses.

Time Estimate: Preparation, 15 minutes; unsupervised, 2 hours

Nutritional Profile per Serving: Calories—72; % calories from fat—0%; fat (gm)—0 or 0% daily value; saturated fat (gm)—0; sodium (mg)—21; cholesterol (mg)—0; carbohydrates (gm)—18; dietary fiber (gm)—2; protein (gm)—2

Autumn Fruit Compote

Serves 6

2 large Bosc pears, peeled, cored, and cut into eighths
4 apricots, halved and pitted, or use 8 dried apricots
2 nectarines, peel on, pitted and cut into eighths
1/4 cup dried tart cherries
1 tablespoon freshly squeezed lemon juice
1 cup de-alcoholized, fruity white wine
1/4 cup packed brown sugar
1/4 teaspoon cinnamon
Pinch of cloves
1 tablespoon arrowroot mixed with 2 tablespoons de-alcoholized white wine (slurry)

Preheat the oven to 350°F (180°C). Combine the fruit in a glass 9 × 13-inch (23 × 33-cm) baking dish. Stir the lemon juice, wine, brown sugar, cinnamon, and cloves together in a small bowl. Pour over the fruit and bake in the preheated oven for 30 to 40 minutes or until the fruit is tender but still holds its shape. Carefully pour the liquid into a saucepan. Stir in the slurry and heat to clear and thicken. This will happen in less than 30 seconds. Pour the thickened sauce back over the fruit and stir to coat. Serve warm or cold.

Time Estimate: Preparation, 15 minutes; unsupervised, 40 minutes

Nutritional Profile per Serving: Calories—123; % calories from fat—7%; fat (gm)—1 or 2% daily value; saturated fat (gm)—0; sodium (mg)—5; cholesterol (mg)—0; carbohydrates (gm)—32; dietary fiber (gm)—3; protein (gm)—1

Kiwis, Oranges, and Lychees in Tonic

Serves 4

 3 kiwifruit, peeled and cut into chunks
 3 medium oranges, peeled and cut into sections
 1 (11-ounce or 312-gm) can lychees, drained
 2 teaspoons finely grated lime zest
 1 cup tonic water

Combine the fruit in a glass bowl, sprinkle with lime zest, and pour tonic over the top. Macerate in the refrigerator for at least 2 hours. Serve in chilled glass dessert dishes or wine glasses.

Time Estimate: Preparation, 20 minutes; unsupervised, 2 hours

Nutritional Profile per Serving: Calories—173; % calories from fat—0%; fat (gm)—0 or 0% daily value; saturated fat (gm)—0; sodium (mg)—6; cholesterol (mg)—0; carbohydrates (gm)—44; dietary fiber (gm)—4; protein (gm)—2

Mint Grapefruit Ice

Serves 6

 1 cup fresh mint leaves and stems
 1/2 cup slightly sweet, fruity wine
 3/4 cup sugar
 2½ cups freshly squeezed pink grapefruit juice
 1 teaspoon finely grated grapefruit zest
 1 tablespoon freshly squeezed lemon juice

Combine the mint, wine, and sugar in a small saucepan and bring to a boil. Cover and set aside, off the heat, for 15 minutes. Strain the liquid into the grapefruit juice and discard the mint. Add the grapefruit zest and lemon juice and pour into the canister of your ice cream freezer. Freeze according to the manufacturer's instructions. For best results, let the ice ripen in the deep freeze for 1 hour before serving. Let it soften slightly before dishing it up.

If you don't have an ice cream machine, freeze the liquid in a baking pan in your freezer until it is almost solid. This will take an hour or two, depending on your freezer.

Break the ice into small pieces and beat with an electric mixer. The more you beat, the smoother the texture will be. One short beating will produce a *granité*. Longer beatings will result in a richer, smoother texture. Freeze again until solid enough to serve.

Time Estimate: Preparation, 15 minutes; cooking, 15 minutes; unsupervised, 1 hour and 20 minutes using an ice cream freezer or 2 to 3 hours in your freezer

Nutritional Profile per Serving: Calories—139; % calories from fat—0%; fat (gm)—0 or 0% daily value; saturated fat (gm)—0; sodium (mg)—3; cholesterol (mg)—0; carbohydrates (gm)—35; dietary fiber (gm)—0; protein (gm)—1

Orange Ice

Serves 6

3 cups freshly squeezed orange juice
2 tablespoons freshly squeezed lemon juice
1 teaspoon orange zest
3/4 cup sugar

Combine all the ingredients and stir until the sugar is completely dissolved. Pour into an ice cream machine and freeze according to the manufacturer's instructions. Allow the ice to ripen in the deep freeze for an hour before serving.

If you don't have an ice cream machine, you may freeze the mixture in a baking pan in the deep freeze. This will probably take up to 2 hours, depending on your freezer. Break up the ice with a wooden spoon and place it in a large bowl. Beat it with an electric mixer until slushy and refreeze. You can serve it at this point or continue beating and freezing until it reaches the smoothness you desire.

Time Estimate: Preparation, 15 minutes; unsupervised, 1 hour and 20 minutes using an ice cream freezer or 2 to 4 hours using a deep freeze

Nutritional Profile per Serving: Calories—154; % calories from fat—0%; fat (gm)—0 or 0% daily value; saturated fat (gm)—0; sodium (mg)—2; cholesterol (mg)—0; carbohydrates (gm)—38; dietary fiber (gm)—0; protein (gm)—1

Basics

Basic Chicken, Turkey, or Duck Stock

Yields 4 cups

1 teaspoon light olive oil with a dash of toasted sesame oil
1 onion, peeled and chopped
1/2 cup coarsely chopped celery tops
1 cup coarsely chopped carrots
Carcass from a whole bird and any meat, fat, or skin scraps
1 bay leaf
2 sprigs fresh thyme
4 sprigs fresh parsley
6 black peppercorns
2 whole cloves

Pour the oil into a large stockpot over medium heat. Add the onion, celery tops, and carrots, and fry to release their volatile oils, about 5 minutes. Add the carcass and seasonings and cover with 8 cups of water. Bring to a boil, reduce the heat, and simmer for 2 to 4 hours, adding water if needed. Skim off any foam that rises to the surface. After 1 hour, add 1 cup of cold water—this will force fat in the liquid to rise to the surface so you can remove it.

Strain; use with relative abandon.

The best way to get rid of excess fat is to chill the stock, let the fat rise to the top and harden, and then pick it off the top.

Basic Beef, Lamb, Ostrich, or Veal Stock

Yields 4 cups

    1 pound (450 gm) beef, lamb, or veal bones, fat trimmed off
    1 teaspoon light olive oil with a dash of toasted sesame oil
    1 onion, peeled and coarsely chopped
    1/2 cup coarsely chopped celery tops
    1 cup coarsely chopped carrots
    1 bay leaf
    2 sprigs fresh thyme
    6 black peppercorns
    2 whole cloves

Preheat the oven to 375°F (190°C). Place the beef, lamb, or veal bones in a roasting pan and cook until nicely browned, about 25 minutes. The browning produces a richer flavor and deeper color in the final stock.

Pour the oil into a large stockpot over medium heat and fry the vegetables for 5 minutes to release their volatile oils. Add the bones and seasonings and cover with 8 cups of water. Bring to a boil, reduce the heat, and simmer 4 to 8 hours, adding more water if necessary. Skim off any foam that rises to the surface. Strain and you've got a marvelous tool.

If you chill the stock in the refrigerator, the fat will harden on top and you will be able to pick it off.

Quick Beef Stock in a Pressure Cooker

Yields 4 cups

Same ingredients as for Basic Beef Stock (above) minus the carrots.

Brown the bones in the oven as for Basic Beef Stock.

Pour the oil into a pressure cooker over medium heat and fry the onion and celery tops for 5 minutes. Add the browned bones and the seasonings and cover with 6 cups of water. Fasten the lid, bring to steam, lower the heat, and cook for 40 minutes from the time when the cooker starts hissing.

Remove from the heat, leave the lid on, and let cool naturally, about 30 minutes. Strain; you will have about 4 cups of stock.

Note: Whenever you're using a pressure cooker, check your manufacturer's instruction book for maximum levels of liquids, etc.

Basic Ham Hock Stock

Yields 6 cups

> 1-pound (450-gm) ham hock
> 1 bay leaf
> 3 whole cloves

In a pressure cooker, cover the ham hock with 2 quarts of cold water. Bring to a boil, remove from the heat, and drain, discarding the water. Put the ham hock back in the pressure cooker and add the bay leaf and cloves. Pour in 2 quarts of fresh, cold water, fasten the lid, and put over the high heat. When the cooker starts hissing, turn the heat down to medium low and let simmer 30 minutes. Carefully skim the fat off the hot soup or chill it thoroughly and pick the hardened fat off the top. Strain and have at it!

Classic Fish or Shrimp Stock

Yields 4 cups

> 1 teaspoon light olive oil with a dash of toasted sesame oil
> 1 onion, peeled and coarsely chopped
> 1/2 cup coarsely chopped celery tops
> 2 sprigs fresh thyme
> 1 bay leaf
> 1 pound fish bones (no heads) or shrimp shells (see Note)
> 6 black peppercorns
> 2 whole cloves

Pour the oil into a large saucepan and sauté the onion, celery tops, thyme, and bay leaf until the onion is translucent—about 5 minutes. To ensure a light-colored stock, be careful not to brown.

Add the fish bones or shrimp shells, peppercorns, and cloves, cover with 5 cups water, bring to a boil, reduce the heat, and simmer for 25 minutes. Strain through a fine-mesh sieve and cheesecloth.

Note: Salmon bones are too strong for fish stocks.

Basic Vegetable Stock

Yields 4 cups

1 teaspoon light olive oil with a dash of toasted sesame oil
1/2 cup coarsely chopped onion
2 cloves garlic, peeled and bashed
1/2 teaspoon freshly grated gingerroot
1/2 cup coarsely chopped carrot
1 cup coarsely chopped celery
1 cup coarsely chopped turnip
1/4 cup coarsely chopped leeks, white and light green parts only
3 sprigs fresh parsley
1/2 teaspoon black peppercorns

Pour the oil into a large stockpot over medium heat, add the onion and garlic, and sauté for 5 minutes. Add the rest of the ingredients and cover with 5 cups of water. Bring to a boil, reduce the heat, and simmer for 30 minutes. Strain, and great flavor is at your fingertips.

Basic Yogurt Cheese

Yields 3/4 cup

1½ cups (354 ml) plain nonfat yogurt, no gelatin added

Put the yogurt in a strainer over a bowl. Or you can use a coffee filter, piece of muslin, or a paper towel and place it in a small sieve over a bowl. Cover and let it drain in the refrigerator for 12 hours or overnight. After 12 hours it becomes quite firm and the small lumps disappear, which makes it ideal for use in sauces. The liquid whey drains into the bowl, leaving you with a thick, creamy yogurt cheese.

Easy, Quick Enhanced Canned Stocks

I let my herb bunches go around twice when I use them to flavor a canned broth. After the first use, put it into a sealable plastic bag and keep it deep-frozen until its next appearance. Do be sure to label it: frozen herb bags could be a disappointing late-night microwave snack for twenty-first-century teenagers!

Canned stock (low-sodium if possible)
Bouquet garni (see below)

Pour the canned stock into a saucepan and add the appropriate bouquet garni. Bring to a boil, reduce the heat, and simmer, uncovered, for 30 minutes. Strain and move forward, enhanced, of course.

Remember: Canned stocks are often loaded with sodium. Please check the label if you are sodium sensitive.

Bouquet Garni

1 bay leaf
2 sprigs fresh thyme, or 1 teaspoon dried
6 black peppercorns
2 whole cloves
3 sprigs parsley

To make a bouquet garni, cut a 4-inch (10-cm) square piece of muslin or cheesecloth, put the ingredients in the center and tie the four corners securely to form a tight pouch. Hit the bouquet garni several times with a mallet or the back of a knife to bruise the herbs and spices, helping them to release their volatile oils.

Variations:

For poultry: Add a 4-inch (10-cm) branch of tarragon (2 teaspoons or 10 ml dried) or 6 sage leaves (1 teaspoon or 5 ml dried).

For fish: Use either a few small branches of fennel or of dill, incorporated into the basic bunch of herbs.

For beef: Use a few branches of marjoram or rosemary incorporated into the basic bunch of herbs.

Basic Pastry Crust

Yields two 8-inch (20-cm) crusts

1½ cups cake flour
1 teaspoon sugar
1/8 teaspoon salt
2 tablespoons light olive oil
4 tablespoons (1/2 stick) margarine or butter, frozen for 15 minutes
1 teaspoon distilled vinegar
4 tablespoons ice water
2 tablespoons 2% milk

Put the flour, sugar, and salt in a large mixing bowl, drizzle evenly with the oil, and whisk together with a fork until it has a fine sandy texture.

Remove the margarine from the freezer and slice it into 1/8-inch (.5-cm) pieces. Stir it into the flour mixture just enough to coat the margarine and keep the pieces from sticking together. Sprinkle with the vinegar and water, then use two knives cutting in a crisscross motion to work the dough just until all the liquid is absorbed. Shape into a ball, put in a small bowl, cover with plastic, and refrigerate for 10 minutes before rolling. The longer it sits, the more the liquid will spread throughout the dough, making it easier to roll. Brush with milk after rolling.

Tips and Hints:

• Use cake flour. It has less protein than all-purpose flour, which reduces the production of gluten and makes for a more tender crust.

• For an even tenderer crust, remove 1 tablespoon of each cup of flour and replace with 1 tablespoon cornstarch. This reduces the protein yet again.

• For sweeter crusts, add more sugar or very sweet fruit purée (like prunes). The sugar prevents gluten from forming by keeping two of the proteins from combining.

• Since my family is trying not to have saturated fat, I use a good solid stick margarine—not the soft tub, which has added water and is difficult to cut into uniform pieces.

Wheat Germ Crust

Covers the top of a 9-inch (23-cm) pie

1½ cups all-purpose flour
1/4 cup wheat germ
6 tablespoons polyunsaturated stick margarine, cut into 12 small pieces and well chilled in the freezer for 2 hours
5 tablespoons ice water
1 tablespoon 2% milk

Sift the flour into a bowl and stir in the wheat germ. Pinch the margarine pieces into the flour with the tips of your fingers until it's completely distributed.

Pour in the ice water and mix the dough with your fingers until it sticks together and forms a small ball.

Preheat the oven to 425°F (220°C). Turn the dough out onto a floured board and roll into a long rectangle, about 1/8 inch (0.5 cm) thick. Fold the bottom third over the middle and the top third over that and repeat the process twice more. Finally, roll the dough out into a circle and place a pie plate on top, upside down. Cut along the outside edge of the pie plate with a sharp knife to get the perfect size circle. Roll it up over the rolling pin and unroll it onto a baking sheet covered with parchment paper. If you're making a pie top with the dough, you might want to score the dough with serving lines that make the crust easier to slice after it's baked. It does make a very crisp, flaky crust. Brush with the milk to glaze. Bake in the preheated oven for 10 minutes.

Salad Dressing Base

Serves 16

1 large yellow onion
1 cup water
1 tablespoon arrowroot
2 tablespoons rice wine vinegar

Cut the onion in half with the skin and ends attached. Lay the halves on a plate, face down, and microwave for 15 minutes. Peel and cut the ends off, place the cooked white part into a blender, and whiz until completely smooth. Push the onion purée through a sieve into a small saucepan. Add the water, arrowroot, and vinegar. Heat to thicken and clear. Cool and use as a base for salad dressings. Store in a covered jar in the refrigerator for up to a week.

Crêpes

reading newspaper headlines through a thin crêpe...

Makes 2 crêpes

1 whole egg
1 egg yolk
1 cup 2% milk
1 cup all-purpose flour
1/2 teaspoon vanilla (for dessert crêpes only)
1 teaspoon extra light olive oil with a dash of sesame oil

In a small bowl, mix the egg, egg yolk, and milk. Sift the flour into another bowl and make a well in the center. Pour the egg mixture into the well and gradually stir together until the flour is fully incorporated. Add the vanilla. Set aside in a cool place and let rest for 30 minutes.

Heat the oil in an 8-inch (20-cm) sauté pan, then pour it into the crêpe batter. This makes the crêpes self-releasing.

Pour 1/4 cup of the batter into the pan and swirl to make a round thin crêpe. Cook until the crêpe becomes slightly brown—approximately 1 minute on each side. Place the cooked crêpes on a plate and cover with a damp towel.

Appendix: Spice Mixes

Spice Mixes

All of the following mixes can be assembled in your own kitchen. The amounts that I've suggested make about 1/2 cup, so you can use them up within a few months.

By using a good, high-speed coffee mill (reserved exclusively for this use), you can powder most but not all herbs and spices. As a final safeguard I pass the powder through a fine sieve before putting it into good ultraviolet-resistant, tightly sealed jars.

Finally, may I recommend that you mark the jar with the date of production and notes on any ingredient changes that appeal to your own flavor preferences.

Shanghai Coastline Ethmix

7 tablespoons crushed red pepper flakes
2¾ teaspoons ground ginger
2¾ teaspoons ground anise

Grind to a fine powder.

Scandinavia Ethmix

4½ teaspoons horseradish powder (wasabi)
2¼ teaspoons caraway seeds
3 tablespoons dried parsley
2¼ teaspoons wild mushroom powder
2¼ teaspoons dried seaweed
1 teaspoon ground white pepper
1/2 teaspoon ground allspice
4¼ teaspoons sea salt

Grind all above to a fine powder and add:

1/2 teaspoon dried dill weed

Northern France Ethmix

10 teaspoons dried tarragon
1¼ teaspoons powdered bay leaf
5 teaspoons dried thyme
1/2 teaspoon ground cloves
10 teaspoons dried chervil

Grind to a fine powder.

Northwest Italy Ethmix

8 teaspoons dried oregano
4 teaspoons dried basil
4 teaspoons ground fennel seeds
4 teaspoons rubbed sage
2 teaspoons dried rosemary

Grind to a fine powder.

Southern France Ethmix

2½ teaspoons dried rosemary
2½ teaspoons dried basil
5 teaspoons rubbed sage
1¼ teaspoons powdered bay leaf
5 teaspoons dried marjoram
5 teaspoons dried oregano

Grind to a fine powder.

Poland Ethmix

4 teaspoons caraway powder
1½ teaspoons dried marjoram
3 whole juniper berries
1/8 teaspoon ground cloves
3/4 teaspoon white pepper

Grind to a fine powder and add:

3 teaspoons dried dill weed

Germany Ethmix

16 whole juniper berries
1 teaspoon dried Cascade hops
1 teaspoon mushroom powder
4 teaspoons dried chives
2 teaspoons horseradish powder (wasabi)
2 teaspoons caraway powder
8 teaspoons dried marjoram
2 teaspoons white pepper

Grind to a fine powder and add:

1/2 teaspoon dried dill weed

Thailand Ethmix

10 teaspoons dried lemon grass
5 teaspoons galangal
1½ teaspoons ground red pepper (cayenne)
1¼ teaspoons dried spearmint
5 teaspoons dried cilantro
2½ teaspoons dried basil

Grind to a fine powder.

India Ethmix

5 teaspoons turmeric
2½ teaspoons dry mustard
5 teaspoons ground cumin
5 teaspoons ground coriander
1¼ teaspoons ground red pepper (cayenne)
2½ teaspoons dill seeds
2½ teaspoons cardamom seeds
2½ teaspoons fenugreek seeds

Grind to a fine powder.

Morocco Ethmix

5 teaspoons grated nutmeg
5 teaspoons ground cumin
5 teaspoons ground coriander
2½ teaspoons ground allspice
2½ teaspoons ground ginger
1¼ teaspoons ground red pepper (cayenne)
1¼ teaspoons ground cinnamon

Grind to a fine powder.

Bali Ethmix

3/4 teaspoon ground bay leaves
4 teaspoons ground ginger
3 teaspoons turmeric
1½ teaspoons dried onion
1½ teaspoons dried garlic
1½ teaspoons freshly ground black pepper
6 teaspoons crushed red pepper flakes

Grind to a fine powder.

Greek Islands Ethmix

4 tablespoons oregano
6 teaspoons ground fennel seeds
6 teaspoons dried lemongrass
3/4 teaspoon black pepper

Grind to a fine powder.

Harissa

3 teaspoons caraway seed
1½ teaspoons cumin
6 teaspoons powdered coriander
12 teaspoons red pepper flakes

Grind to a fine powder.

Index

Cabernet sauce, roast ostrich with tart cherry, 86–87
Cajun MEV with black-eyed peas and collard greens, 138–39
Canadian bacon
 roasted peppers and cheese on a muffin, 44
 savory waffles, 38
canned beans, 46–47
cannellini, Italian MEV with artichokes and, 133
cantaloupe
 cooking with, 187
 Italian MEV with cannellini and artichokes, 133
 salad, 26
 sparkling melon with strawberries, 200
carrots
 baby, steamed, 152
 lamb vegetable curry, 106
 mixed rice vegetable pilaf, 164
 ostrich neck soup with vegetables and mushrooms, 16–17
 and parsnips, grated, 156
 penne with Italian sausage and sugar peas, 92–93
 Peruvian tofu and vegetables, 127
 steamed chicken strips with, 79
 in tonic water, 152
casserole, chicken noodle, 82–83
catfish
 with Creole quinoa, 68–69
 farmed, 67
cauliflower, steamed, 153
cedar plank, 52–53
 pork tenderloin with apples and onions on a, 107
cedar-roasted vegetable sandwich, 54
Cervena, 111
chayote squash, in South American vegetable soup, 18
Cheddar cheese, nonfat, in white bean and green chili quesadillas, 50
cheese
 Canadian bacon and roasted peppers on a muffin, 44
 panini with peas, sun-dried tomatoes and olives, 43
 panini with prosciutto and fennel, 42
 savory waffles, 38
 shrimp and rice frittata, 34
 Treena's square eggs, 33
 white bean and green chili quesadillas, 50
 yogurt. see yogurt cheese

cherries
 cooking with, 184
 tart, Cabernet sauce, roast ostrich with, 86–87
chicken
 bouquet garni for, 211
 breast MEV Shanghai, 74–75
 handling, 73
 noodle casserole, 82–83
 roasted, 73
 stock, basic, 207
 strips with carrots, steamed, 79
chick peas (garbanzo beans)
 MEV, Moroccan orange, 134–35
 on pita, Moroccan, 48
chili, green, and white bean quesadillas, 50
chutney yogurt sauce, for dal MEV, 132
cinnamon apple frozen yogurt, 178–79
clay pylon bakers, 70, 72
collard greens
 bean soup with sausage and mushrooms, 22–23
 Cajun MEV with black-eyed peas and, 138–39
 Polish MEV with apples and beets, 139
 steamed, 153
 steamed mixed greens, 154
compote, fruit
 autumn, 201
 tropical, 200
convection ovens, 70–71
corn
 baby, stir-fried pork with pea pods and, 110
 Shanghai stuffed peppers, 144
 with tamari and lime juice, roasted, 160
 tomato vegetable soup with sweet potato, 14
couscous
 MEV, North African pea soup with a, 15
 with mint, 158
cranberries, cooking with, 185
cranberries, dried
 fruity wild rice, 165
 sautéed turkey breast with fennel, mushrooms, and pears, 96–97
Creole quinoa, catfish with, 68–69
crêpes, 214
crispy cups, sautéed nashi in, 193
crust
 basic pastry, 212
 wheat germ, 213

cucumber
 and apple salad, 25
 Mexican, 27
currant jelly–wild mushroom sauce, rack of venison with, 113
curry, lamb vegetable, 106

dal MEV with yogurt chutney sauce, 132
dates, cooking with, 185
delicata squash
 catfish with creole quinoa, 68–69
 cedar-roasted vegetable sandwich, 54
dessert
 apples as, 183
 apricots as, 183
 Asian pears as, 183
 autumn fruit compote, 201
 baked ginger pineapple, 198
 baked peach slices, 199
 bananas as, 184
 bananas with pineapple sauce, 194
 blackberries as, 184
 blueberries as, 184
 broiled apricots with almonds, 197
 cherries as, 184
 cinnamon apple frozen yogurt, 178–79
 cranberries as, 185
 dates as, 185
 figs as, 185
 grapefruit as, 185
 grapes as, 186
 kiwifruit as, 186
 kiwis, oranges, and lychees in tonic, 202
 lychees as, 186
 mangoes as, 186
 melons as, 187
 mint grapefruit ice, 202–3
 nectarines as, 187
 orange ice, 203
 oranges as, 187
 papaya as, 187
 peaches as, 188
 pears as, 188
 pineapple as, 188
 plums as, 188
 poached rhubarb sauce with blueberries over orange sections, 195
 prunes as, 189
 raspberries as, 189
 raspberry Pavlova with berry sauce, 180–81
 rhubarb as, 189
 sautéed nashi in crispy cups, 193

Let's Stay In Touch!

Dear Reader,

Thank you so much for taking the time to read this book—all the way to the back cover!

I've been especially thrilled to bring you these recipes and hints for an exciting and healthy way of making food that's both delicious and good for you!

If you'd like to be part of the continuing process, please drop me a line with your comments and send it with the form below—or just send in the completed form so that I can get back to you with updates on new ideas, recipes, and culinary products.

From my kitchen to yours,

With love and thanks,

Graham

Graham Kerr

Detach and mail to: The Kerr Corporation, P.O. Box 1598, Dept. F, Stanwood, WA 98292

"I want to stay in touch!"

YES! I want to stay in touch and receive information about new ideas and products from Graham Kerr.

Please check: ☐ Under 40
☐ 40-59
☐ Over 60

My Name _____

Address _____

City _____ State/Zip _____

Phone Number (Optional): (_____) _____
Area Code

MAIL TO: The Kerr Corporation, P.O. Box 1598, Dept. F, Stanwood, WA 98292